According To Eve

Living and loving in the early 1950s

© Milla Reed 2025

First published 2025

Front cover by DAM Design Creative Ltd

Published by

CareerTrain Publishing

careertrainbooks@gmail.com

All rights reserved. No part of this publication may be reproduced or utilised in any form or by any means, electronic or mechanical, or stored in an information retrieval system (other than for purposes of review) without the express permission of the Careertrain Publishing in writing.

Note: The material contained in this book is set out in good faith for general guidance only. While the author has used their best efforts in preparing this book, they make no representations or warranties with respect to the accuracy or completeness of the contents of this book. Every effort has been made to trace the copyright holders of material in this book. If application is made in writing to the publisher, any omissions will be included in future editions.

According To Eve

Living and loving in the early 1950s

MILLA REED

Careertrain Publishing

Contents

Part One:

The time, people and place   Page 7

Part Two:

The diaries with notes   Page 25

Part Three:

What happened to Eve, Reg and Fred?   Page 153

Appendix:

How to be a mind reader   Page 167

About the Author   Page 170

Acknowledgements   Page 171

Part One: The time, place and people

A secret in the wardrobe...

What you are about to read is a true account - or at least as true as any personal diary. These entries reveal an emotional period for my mum, Eve, shedding light on her life in 1950s Kent, and about her inner turmoil as she's torn between her two great loves.

The diaries. Each one measures ten by six centimetres.

Eve died in 2011. Clearing out her house afterwards, I came across two small leatherbound pocket diaries. They were tucked away among half-finished and abandoned sewing projects in the wardrobe of her box room. There were no other mementoes nearby. They measure ten by six centimetres (four by two and a half inches), one red, one black, from 1951 and 1952. The tiny writing is in ink from a fountain pen, often smudged or feathered, making it hard to read. I'd never known Mum write for pleasure or reflection. I browsed through them, picking out sentences where I could.

I stored the diaries with Eve's other documents and returned to my task of fulfilling my role as executor for her estate. There was a lot to do. It was twelve years before I came across them again and remembered I intended to type them up. I didn't expect to find anything new but set about the task, often turning to Twitter/X users for help in deciphering the words. My phone was incredibly useful too. I photographed pages, enlarged them, and cropped them so I could concentrate on each mystery I was trying to solve. Between me, my phone, and the lovely Twitter/X community, pretty much everything became clear. And I discovered plenty.

According to Eve

The Time

There are two stories in Eve's diaries. Firstly, the personal one. The entries are mainly factual accounts of her days. Comments like '*Work as usual. Washed my hair*' pop up a lot, so don't expect it all to be riveting reading; much of it is mundane but do persevere. Woven through the trivialities is the heartbreak of losing her first love, Fred, and learning to live without him. Eventually she finds happiness again when she meets my father, Reg, but life throws another curveball when her parents announce that they are selling up and moving away, leaving her homeless and feeling abandoned at the age of twenty. With a new job and a new love, her only option was to find local lodgings. Her parent's decision affected her deeply, perhaps because it echoed the pain of Fred leaving her, or her experience of being evacuated as a small child during the second world war.

Evacuation was a scheme to protect children from bombs. Eve was sent to live in the country with her sister, Pamela, but without her parents. Not fully understanding why you were separated from your mother and father, and not knowing if you would ever see them again, was a traumatising experience. Mum was a strong, resilient woman but I believe the memories of feeling abandoned by her parents (twice) and Fred remained with her. You will need to read between the lines, but it is easy to do. My guess is that the sparse entries served to remind her of significant events and how they unfolded.

When the diaries begin, it had been six years since World War two ended. Both Eve and Fred would have lived through it from the ages of seven to thirteen, a significant and formative chunk of their childhood, so no doubt it impacted them greatly.

Reg, being six years older, would have been thirteen when the war broke out and nineteen when it ended, so it encompassed all his teen years. Many of the young people mentioned would have had fathers who had been called up to fight.

There was conscription in place at the time – the scheme where young men had no choice but to do national Service for eighteen months, so the military still cast a long shadow. There is mention of Fred and others serving in the armed forces, but not Reg. If my memory serves me correctly, I believe that Reg fulfilled his spell in the UK at a different time, possibly earlier, as he was older. I remember hearing that he had been sent down coal mines.

The second story, a vivid portrait of how young people lived in post war Britain, is astounding. In addition to the stories of love and friendship, the casual descriptions seem to take for granted cinemas, dance halls, music, theatre and social occasions almost every week. If you wanted to go dancing this weekend, with a live band in a hall, would you be able to find somewhere near you? And would you be able to easily afford it? Would there be cheap buses and trains if you needed them? If you went to London's West End to see famous actors in a show, what proportion of your weekly income would it take? All the characters in Eve's diaries were working class, yet they seemed to have access to it all. It would be understandable that they were determined to live life to the full after the frugality and terror of the years at war. Entertainment appeared to be inexpensive and abundant.

The cost of West End theatre tickets in 1951 ranged from five to twenty five shillings, which equates to between £2 and £15 today. Actual prices today range from about £22.50 to £300 so yes, theatre was much more affordable in Eve's day. Cinema tickets were, on average, just under eight shillings, which equates to £2.81 in today's money. In 2025, we are paying around £8, roughly three times as much.

    I had a distant memory of a photo album with pictures of that era, mainly featuring Mum on motorbikes – but I hadn't seen it since I was a teenager. Eventually my sister tracked it down in her son's attic, so I've been able to match up some diary entries with photographs, despite many of them having no writing or labels to help me. Many of them are tiny, only about five centimetres square. One surprise was that there is a photo or a group of friends, taken in Rochester Castle Gardens in 1947, that has both Eve and Fred in it, so they knew each other when they were fifteen. My guess is that they began dating when they were sixteen, so they had been together for four years when they broke up.

According to Eve

1947. Eve captioned this *'Taken one Sunday morning in Castle Gardens on the way home from the swimming baths'*. Eve is on the left, Fred is third from the right. The couple in the middle appear to have swapped jackets, the lad on the right is wearing his back to front!

The People

Here's an introduction to the main characters:

Eve Reed

Eve was born on 16th January 1932, a second daughter for Alfred and Doris. She was christened Evelyn but was always known as Eve. She attended Chatham Grammar School for Girls – the same school as me – gaining a qualification known as matriculation, which was the precursor to the O and A level system.

She was intelligent and quick witted, but university wasn't a viable option. Eve often expressed regret that she had not been able to go. At the time, it was fiercely competitive, and costs were high. Her parents would not have been able to afford it, and of course, it wasn't a normal thing for the working classes to do. Only 3.4% of young people went to university compared to 38% these days. She had a thirst for learning which is evident in her night school education and the qualifications she went on to gain in later life. Instead, she took a job as a clerk in a firm of solicitors in London (B & Rs), which meant commuting by train.

According to Eve

This picture was taken by a street photographer in Nice, when Eve was on holiday in France in 1952. She was twenty years old.

Eve's parents

Alfred Reed and Doris Du Mont's wedding in Camden, 1927. They were Eve's parents.

The family lived in Napier Road, Gillingham. Her father, Alfred, was a quiet, good looking man with heavy eyebrows and a quick sense of humour. He worked as an electrician for the South Eastern Electricity Board. I have few memories of him as he died from lung cancer in 1967 when I was nine. He was sixty three when he died.

Her mother, Doris, was a housemaid before she married. A plain woman, she blamed her figure on 'fat being absorbed through her skin' while working below stairs in kitchens. Doris was a good cook – a skill passed on to Pam, Eve's sister, but not to Eve, who was far less interested in domestic skills, with the exception of sewing. She enjoyed making clothes.

Doris's father was French and her mother half French. I have no recollection of her having any interest in France at all, but it may explain Eve's abiding love of the country. I was surprised that there was no criticism of Doris in the diaries. She had a sharp tongue, often nagging or complaining. As children, my sister and I were sent to her for a couple of weeks each summer, so I had firsthand experience of this. Maybe Eve was concerned that her mother might read her diary?

Doris was always fond of card games – there is mention of Whist drives and Newmarket in the diaries – and this often involved a 'flutter'; she enjoyed it more when money was at stake. In later years she became a stalwart at the bingo hall.

Pamela Cornish née Reed

Pamela was Eve's older sister, who worked as a secretary. Pam and Eve were both chatterboxes, although Pam was possibly worse than Eve. They used to hold conversations where it was entirely normal for them both to talk at the same time for the duration.

At the time of the diaries, Pam was a young bride, having married Maurice, a welder and boilermaker who worked on ships at Chatham Dockyard, in 1949. They are often mentioned as P&M.

From left to right: Maurice and Pam with Fred and Eve at a dance circa 1950.

Fred Wanless

Fred Wanless was the handsome, dark haired son of Fred and Emily Wanless, who lived in Dale Street, Chatham. He was Eve's first love and the same age as her, so he too was only nineteen when the diaries commence. His son describes him as a thoughtful and sensitive man who enjoyed the company of others (especially women!)

He had a great interest in motorbikes, perhaps because they helped him get to social events. He trained as a carpenter and never lost his appreciation of finely crafted wood. He also spent time in the forces. Fred had one sister, Audrey.

According to Eve

This was taken just before Fred joined the army in 1952 for his National Service. He was stationed in Malaya, which is now known as Peninsular Malaysia.

Reg Thrush

Reg with Eve in 1952

Reg was born on 11th January 1926. He was my father, the only son of Alice and George Thrush. George was a carpenter who had also served in the armed forces. As a child, Reg spent some time living in Gibraltar when his father was deployed there. When they returned to England, they lived in Burnt Oak Terrace, Gillingham. Alice and George remained there until their old age. Reg was left handed. In those days, this was seen as a fault, and he was forced to write with his right hand. The upshot was that his handwriting became completely illegible whichever hand he used!

Reg's abiding passion was for music. He was a talented singer. He used a stage name – Johnny Miller – as he didn't think 'Reg Thrush' would appeal to audiences. If he wasn't singing or playing percussion, he would be listening to jazz or talking about it. Reg was a well-liked, good natured man who had a friendly remark or joke for everyone. This made him a good front man for the bands he played with. He was working in a High Street tobacconist shop in 1951. He was six years older than Eve, so would have been twenty five at the time of the diaries. In later life he did administrative work and continued to sing semi-professionally until health prevented him.

✦✦✦✦✦

There are many more friends and relations mentioned below. You'll come across Arthur and Betty (sometimes referred to as A&B). Their daughter Lynn has provided additional pictures. I've not been able to solve all the questions raised. I can't work out quite how many Allans/Alans there are – at least two, although I'm leaning towards three. There are two different Joans - one is a work colleague and friend, the other dates Fred after Eve. I'd love to know who Carol was, because the language is slightly different around her. Eve says she takes her out, rather than going out with her, so maybe it was a friend or neighbour with a disability. There had been epidemics of polio at this time so this may have been a possibility.

The Place

All the families lived in turn of the century modest, turn-of-the-century terraced houses. Both the Wanlesses and Thrushes had outside lavatories – I don't know about the Reeds. The Wanlesses installed an inside toilet in the early 1960's, but the Thrushes (my grandparents) never did. I used the outhouse as a child and remember being washed in a tin bath in front of the coal fire. Their home was small, with a long narrow garden separated from the back door by an alley that ran past the back of all the neighbours so that back doors and gardens could be accessed.

The setting for Eve's diaries is The Medway Towns – the collective name for three towns, Rochester, Chatham and Gillingham, so called because they are set around the River Medway. These three towns are about thirty miles from London and over the years they have grown into each other. Chatham and Gillingham have strong armed forces connections. Chatham Dockyard, built, repaired and refitted Royal Navy ships. It was a major employer locally. Gillingham had army barracks that were home for The Royal Engineers. Rochester is more famous for its historical connections. It has a fine Norman castle and many town centre buildings that date back to the fourteenth century, and of course, it was the home of Charles Dickens.

Reg and Eve lived less than a mile from each other in Gillingham. Fred, in Chatham, was a couple of miles away. The Good Companions Club, which features a lot in the 1952 diary, was in an imposing position at the top of Star Hill in Rochester. This was around two and a half miles from Eve's house. It is notable, not only because of the many times it crops up, but also because it is unlike any other club I've known. Founded by Frank Taylor in 1935, it was originally called The Gay Venturers. Frank and his friends wanted a place where they could get together to play sport and take part in other recreational activities, such as drama, music, dancing and putting on variety shows. The club was born and was very successful, attracting young adults. Members paid a subscription and could pay extra to join different sections of the club. They acquired the building at the top of Star Hill that was the home to many of their social activities, but the main hall there was not large enough to stage shows or dances with bands, so they often used other venues nearby. Sports happened off site as well. You'll find Arthur and Betty mentioned many times in the diaries. Arthur was also a founding member of the club and both he and Betty were good friends with Eve, offering her a room when her parents moved away.

There are many other venues mentioned too. Most are long past their original use – some demolished, some repurposed – but some buildings, such as Chatham Town Hall, remain. The dances, cinemas and theatres may be long gone, but if you want to immerse yourself in the era, there are many references to films, coupled with Mum's opinion, ranging from 'utter tripe' to 'jolly good'. I certainly plan to watch some of them.

Nearby towns and villages come up as well, usually when there were outings on motorbikes. Ramsgate, where her parents relocate, is a popular seaside town on The Isle of Thanet, near Margate and Broadstairs.

The true story

What follows is a complete transcript of the diaries. If a sentence doesn't make sense, or stops midway, or has a blank space in it, or a misspelling, that is how Eve wrote it. There are many gaps in 1951, but 1952 is more complete. I've added notes in italics to tell you a bit more about the events and places Eve mentions, where I could find information. Some I could not trace, others revealed a rich seam of history.

The first diary entry is on 16th January 1951, Eve's nineteenth birthday. It's a happy day. She has a party with good friends, including Fred. There are lots of presents too. Contrast it with the same date the following year – you'll find her alone with five cards and a pair of nylons. She is miserable and cries. Some things never change, and losing your first love is always painful.

After the diaries, I'll tell you what became of Eve, Reg and Fred. You might need tissues.

1951 – 1952: The Diaries

1951

TUES 16 JANUARY (Eve's nineteenth birthday)

My birthday - had a party and invited Fred, Doreen and John, Shirley and Tony, Yvonne and Arthur, P&M. It went very well. I had some lovely presents including 3 headsquares.

Fred is Eve's boyfriend. P&M are Pam and Maurice, her elder sister and husband.

FRI 2 FEBRUARY

Should have gone to show with Eric but didn't – came home early – Fred came over – but I went to bed early. Wish I had gone now.

SAT 3 FEBRUARY

Went to Joan's 21st birthday party. All the gang bought her a dressing table set hand worked on the back. Very good party. Stayed the night with Audrey.

A dressing table set was usually a matching hairbrush, clothes brush and a mirror, sometimes presented on a tray.
'Handworked' will have referred embroidered patterns, usually floral, that were on the back of the items.

Sun 4 February

Pouring with rain. Stayed to dinner at Freds. Then went home and came back to watch TV

Tues 6 February

Fred's birthday. I will buy him a present on Saturday. Watched TV in evening – a good show.

It was Fred's nineteenth birthday.

Weds 7 February

Night school as usual. Have got to take an exam in May for book-keeping. New season today.

Thurs 8 February

Night school for French. Mr Carr said I am improving in my speaking.

Fri 9 February

Pam's birthday – I gave her a white blouse with coffee lace on it – she made a lovely cake for the office.

Sat 10 February

Went to work in the morning + Mr Rawley & Mr King came in. Doreen's birthday - gave her a makeup bag full of things. Saw Eric.

It was common for clerical staff to work on Saturdays in this era. Most jobs were for forty eight hours a week, with around sixteen days leave a year.

SUN 11 FEBRUARY

Gave Fred his stop lights for a birthday present & we went to his house for a birthday tea – had some very strong sherry. Came home on John's bike.

Not all motorbikes were fitted with brake lights as standard in 1951. It became compulsory to have them in 1955.

Fred and Eve. Eve is sitting on Fred's bike, a 1950 AJS 16MC, which was a 350cc single cylinder.

Mon 12 February

Work as usual – stayed in in evening. Fred came over.

Tues 13 February

Same as yesterday – Dad showed us his box of magic in evening – very amusing. Was sick in evening. Eaten too much I suppose.

Weds 14 February

Work as usual – didn't go to night school but had an early night. Had a Valentine telegram from Fred.

To send a telegram, Fred would have either visited a Post Office or telephoned the Central Post Office. He would have told them exactly what words he wanted on the telegram. As the cost was calculated per word, messages were usually brief. It was typed into a teleprinter and then delivered by a telegraph boy on a cycle or motor bike.

Thurs 15 February

Work then went to Doreens and on to night school. Fred didn't meet me. Told me later that he'd had a blackout at work.

Fri 16 February

Stayed in in evening. There is nothing worth seeing at flicks. Very boring evening. F and I played cards and listened to radio. I am very fed up.

Sat 17 February

Pouring with rain today again. Did some shopping for Mum in the morning.

Sun 18 February

Stayed in bed late & went to Mr & Mrs Wanless' for tea & watched television. Saw the play 'The Ambassador' it was very good.

Eve got the name wrong here – the play on TV (only BBC was available at the time) was a farce called The Magistrate, adapted from the 1884 play by Arthur Wing Pinero. It was a tale of widow who married a Magistrate, lied about her age, and persuaded her nineteen year old son to pretend he was fourteen, which causes mayhem as she is not aware that he smokes, flirts and gambles!

Mon 19 February

Went to work as usual. Fred didn't come over in evening he had an attack of hay fever. So I stayed in and went to bed early.

Tues 20 February

Went to pictures in the evening and saw 'Tarzan and the Slave Girl. It was quite good but not really my type of film.

Tarzan and the Slave Girl was an American adventure film, the fourteenth in the Tarzan series. Lex Barker played Tarzan. He was the third actor to take the role, following Johnny Weissmuller.

Weds 21 February

Work in daytime then I went to night school for bookkeeping. The master told me off for talking too much.

THURS 22 FEBRUARY

Work as usual then night school for French. We read about Paris – how I would love to go there.

FRI 23 FEBRUARY

Stayed in in the evening – we are going to save up for our holiday. Fred says he will be able to manage one week in France. Will see Mr Carr about it next Thursday.

The norm at the time was to visit holiday camps within the UK, such as Butlins and Pontins. These became popular in the 1930s, but many were turned over to military use during the war. Most were returned to their original use, with newspapers reporting that the holidaymakers marched in as the soldiers marched out. Seaside boarding houses were popular too.

Holidays abroad were a rarity, especially for the working classes. Only 2% of the population travelled abroad in 1950. Package holidays were available, but travel was usually by train. Passenger jets were introduced in the 1960's.

Eve always felt a strong affinity with France and felt at home there. Although her mother was born in London, her grandfather was French and his wife was half French. In later years, Eve owned a small holiday gîte and spent her summers in the Vendee region, not far from the coast.

SAT 24 FEBRUARY

Didn't get up till 11 o'clock. Took Carol out in the afternoon. Spent boring evening in with Fred. We had no money and nothing to do & I wouldn't go and watch the television – I got so bored with it.

Sun 25 February

Helped Mum in morning and Auntie Kath & Auntie Maisie, David, James, Fred, Pam and Maurice came to tea. We played cards in the evening. Auntie Maisie is very nice. 1st time I have seen her.

Mon 26 February

Just for a change stayed in in the evening. Mum went to W.D per usual & Dad stayed in. Fred left early & caught bus home.

WD is a whist drive, a popular social event where participants would play a hand of whist (a card game) at a small table, then progress up or down to other tables depending on whether they had won or lost.

Tues 27 February

Stayed in in evening & mucked about with my yellow dress – I don't know what to do with it. I don't like the neckline. Went to bed quite early.

Weds 28 February

Work as usual and night school as usual in evening. Fred surprised me by meeting me on his bike – it isn't taxed yet.

Thurs 1 March

Work then night school as usual. Mrs Garrod's hall light had conked out. I must ask Dad to see to it for her if he has time.

Mrs Garrod was her friend Doreen's mother.

According to Eve

Fri 2 March

Pay day – Hurrah! Went to see 'Born to be Bad' + 'Where Danger Lives' Both pretty good films but first one too much like 'All About Eve' – same story.

'Born to be Bad' was based on Ann Parrish's 1928 novel 'All Kneeling'. It was a film noir melodrama about a woman who will stop at nothing to get what she wants.

'All About Eve' was based on a 1946 short story by Mary Orr. It starred Bette Davis as an ageing Broadway star.

https://creativecommons.org/licenses/by/2.0

Sat 3 March

Stayed in bed all morning & went out shopping in afternoon. How bored I am with life – I am fed up with nowhere to go.

Sun 4 March

Went to tea with the Wanless's & then went to see Audrey off. Mrs W and Audrey parted with tears & God know what else as if she was going to China instead of to London.

Audrey was going to stay in a hostel in London, probably to be nearer work.

Mon 5 March

Stayed in evening & washed my hair. Then went to bed early.

Tues 6 March

Met Audrey in evening & spent it at her hostel – it is a beautiful place just like an A1 hotel!!

A1 was a phrase used to describe something of high quality.

Weds 7 March

Night school again for bookkeeping – it is getting very hard now.

Thurs 8 March

French night school – Fred met me & stayed quite late I caught the train home.

WEDS 21 MARCH

Night school in evening – I don't think I shall ever pass the exam in bookkeeping – it really is very hard.

THURS 22 MARCH

Last night at night school for 3 weeks – Fred met me on his bike – he's happy as a sand boy.

GOOD FRIDAY 23 MARCH

Stayed in all day & in the evening as there is nothing worth seeing on pictures & a lousy programme on TV. Fred had to work all day.

SAT 24 MARCH

Went out with Mum and we bought some distemper for my room and a new satin walnut dressing table which they delivered in p.m.

Distemper was a form of whitewash, giving a chalky finish that allowed walls to breathe and moisture to escape. Emulsion paint was invented in the 1940s, but at this time it was at least five times more expensive than distemper.

Satin Walnut is the wood from the American Red Gum tree – no relation to a Walnut tree.

EASTER SUNDAY 25 MARCH

Went to watch TV with Wanless's and watched TV in P.M. It was an awful play!

The play was an adaptation of Cranford by Mrs Gaskell. Described as 'gentle comedy portraying the mundane lives of old spinsters,' the 1853 novel was originally published in episodes in 'Household Words' magazine. After the first article, the editor of the magazine saw potential and encouraged Mrs Gaskell to write more episodes. That editor was Charles Dickens.

EASTER MONDAY 26 MARCH

Helped Dad to paint my room in morning – in p.m. saw boat race on TV & watched it for rest of evening. A good show.

The Boat Race is an annual event on The River Thames between the universities of Cambridge and Oxford. This was the 97th race which Cambridge won.

TUES 27 MARCH

Back to work! Stayed in in evening washed my hair & had a bath + read 'Good Wives'.

Good Wives was Louisa May Alcott's sequel to her famous novel 'Little Women.'

WEDS 28 MARCH

Work as usual – missed 5.42 & had to catch 6.07. Fred was waiting for me & by the time I got ready it was too late to go anywhere.

THURS 29 MARCH

Went to flicks & saw 'The Battle of Powder River'. Quite good as Indian movies go.

'The Battle of Powder River' was known as *'Tomahawk'* in the USA. It was one of the first films that empathised with native Americans.

Fri 30 March

Work as usual – went for a ride in evening – found a nice little café in Sittingbourne – must go there again – it was very cold tonight but not raining thank goodness.

Sat 31 March

I didn't feel very well so I stayed in in evening & Fred came over. I couldn't get warm. I went out in pm and bought pair of grey slacks.

Sun 1 April

Stayed in bed until lunchtime & we went to tea with Auntie Nellie and Uncle Len. Played cards in evening and I won 2/6. Fred went straight home & I caught bus home with Mum and Dad.

Mon 2 April

Had letter from Auntie Jessie asking me to go & see her. She is still staying with Marjorie she fell and hurt her back. Stayed in evening & Fred came over.

Sun 8 April

Went to Doreens for the day & I gave her a home perm. It took all night. Went to Wanlesses in evening and watched television.

Home perms, or permanent waves, were all the rage. Strong smelling ammonia based chemicals were applied to the hair, which was sectioned into small parts. Each part was wrapped round a plastic roller and held in place with a pin. After a set time, the hair was rinsed and conditioner applied. Kits were sold in boxes that contained everything you needed.

'Perm' is short for permanent – the curls remained until the hair grew out.

WEDS 11 APRIL

Night school – went as usual. Nothing in particular happened today.

Night school was held at Chatham Technical School for Girls, which was a few minutes' walk from Chatham station. It is now Fort Pitt Grammar School.

THURS 12 APRIL

Went to Mrs Garrod's from the station & decided not to go to night school so I stayed there. Met Fred outside night school at 9pm.

SAT 14 APRIL

Went to flicks in evening & saw 'Manon'. Mum has been in bed all day so I have had to do cooking shopping & cleaning.

'Manon' was an award winning drama about a bitter relationship between a frivolous girl and a French Resistance soldier.

Sun 15 April

Mum got up today in time for lunch. I went for a ride in the afternoon with Fred. We ended up at Maidstone Zoo. Watched TV in evening.

Maidstone Zoo was the largest privately owned zoo of its time. It was opened to the public in 1934 and became popular with the public and celebrities. It closed in 1959.

Mon 16 April

Work as usual – auditors came in p.m. Stayed in in evening. Had a bit of a cold. Mum was well enough to go to her whist drive.

Tues 17 April

Went to Mrs Garrods for dinner last night & set Doreen's hair in evening. Fred and John came round. Stayed quite late talking.

A 'set' was not the same as a perm -it was a similar process of wrapping wet hair round curlers but only lasted until the hair was washed. A setting lotion was used to hold the curls in place.

Weds 18 April

Night school – book-keeping – I am fed up with the silly old bloke of a master – he keeps explaining simple things & rushing over the things I don't understand.

Thurs 19 April

Work as usual. I have nothing to do, the auditors have all my books.

FRI 20 APRIL

Fort Pitt KEC exam 7pm. I didn't do at all well. Mr Fuller helped me with my balance sheet.

KEC was Kent Education Committee

SAT 21 APRIL

Did a bit of shopping in pm. Bought a couple of pairs of socks & a suspender belt. Went to flicks in evening.

Most women were still wearing stockings, which require a suspender belt or corset to hold them up. Although tights were available from the 1940s, they didn't overtake stockings in popularity until the 1970s.

SUN 22 APRIL

Went out for a ride in p.m – it was a nice day – went to East Farleigh then on to Yalding – laddered my best nylons!

MON 23 APRIL

Went for a ride in evening to   . It was very nice and there is a nice pub there. Bought some raffle tickets for the fete at Whitsun.

I assume Eve forgot the name of the place and intended to write it in the gap when she remembered.

TUES 24 APRIL

Fred said he would let me know definitely about the holiday today – but he didn't come over. I will tell Mrs Tabel we can't go.

WEDS 25 APRIL

Sent wire to Mrs Tabel. Was cross with Fred when he came over. I won't go away for a holiday now. It's too late to book up. Went to night school.

A 'wire' was a telegraph or telegram – as Fred sent Eve on Valentine's Day. It was a popular form of communication before telephones were freely available. Eve mentions Reg phoning her in September 1952, so they probably had a phone at home by then.

THURS 26 APRIL

Went to flicks in evening – quite a good film. Dad ordered his Bantam today. He should have it on the road next week.

A BSA Bantam was a small motorbike, the engine would have been between 125 – 175cc, so not very powerful. Eve always remembered it fondly.

TUES 22 MAY

Went to dinner with Shirley and stayed the evening. Iris has a lorry in tomorrow's carnival. There was a last minute rush on.

According to Eve

WEDS 23 MAY

Got off train at Chatham and watched the carnival – a very good effort. Watched fireworks at football grounds afterwards.

FRI 1 JUNE

Went to see the Strood Methodist Players in 'Maritana' in evening with Fred. It was terribly amateur and the seats were very hard. Went to bed quite early.

Maritana was a three act opera that was first produced in Theatre Royal in Drury Lane in 1845.

SAT 2 JUNE

Went to Festival South Bank in a.m. & went round Tower of London in p.m. & to see 'Kiss Me Kate' in Colosseum in evening. I liked it a lot and so did Audrey & Ross & John. Fred and Molly weren't very keen on it.

The Festival of Britain was a national exhibition, funded by the government. Visited by millions, its goals were to show that there had been a successful recovery from the devastation of war, and promote British achievements in science, technology, and the arts.

'Kiss Me, Kate' is Cole Porter's musical comedy based on William Shakespeare's 'Taming of the Shrew.' It had premiered at The Colosseum in March and ran for 400 performances.

SUN 3 JUNE

Tired after yesterday so lazed in garden in a.m. Went rowing with Audrey and John p.m.& stayed in in evening.

Sat 9 June

Went to London in a.m with Gerry to get her a sundress – didn't get one. Went to Arthur and Yvonne's engagement party in the evening – had a very nice time.

Sun 10 June

Went to Seasalter for the day – wanted to go swimming but no one would come with me so I just sunbathed all day.

Seasalter is a coastal village, near the Estuary of the River Medway.

Mon 11 June

Fred said he had to know definitely if John and Doreen were coming on holiday with us. He went round to see them but they were out.

Tues 12 June

Doreen and John came round in evening but we had gone to the pictures. Saw 'The Browning Version'. I thought it was jolly good.

'The Browning Version' was based on Terence Rattigan's play about a retiring school master. It starred Michael Redgrave.

Weds 13 June

Doreen and John came round for the evening – we made arrangements for the holiday. Made Freddy a carpenter's apron because his old one was worn out.

According to Eve

SAT 16 JUNE

Did home perm for Pam. She made me go home for dinner – had to rush to get dressed. She wanted to go to the pageant at Rochester Castle Gardens.

This pageant was supported by the Festival of Britain. A tribute to Charles Dickens, it contains eleven 'episodes' – short plays or sketches. It was opened by the Mayor of London but wasn't the success expected. Tickets cost between five shillings and one pound one shilling, which was expensive for the time. The event had catered for an audience of up to 85,000 people, but only 19,000 attended, leading to a loss of £6,181 (equivalent to around £236,000 today), only £3,358 of which was covered by the guarantee from The Festival of Britain.

Undeterred, Rochester continued to have Dickens themed events. Hopefully the finances balance better!

SUN 17 JUNE

Went out for the day to a place called Peacehaven – near Newhaven and Brighton – with John and Joan. Quite a nice day – got very brown but not warm enough for swimming.

MON 18 JUNE

Fred came round in evening to see if I had forgotten about the play tomorrow night.

TUES 19 JUNE

Went to see 'Nicholas Nickleby' in Castle Gardens – part of Dickens Festival – it poured with rain and we couldn't hear what was being said.

Fri 22 June

Shirely came to dinner and we sat gassing all evening. She said she will do me a home perm before my holiday.

Sat 23 June

Went shopping for Mum in a.m. Saw them off at 2.30pm. Bill took them in his car. Went to Joyces for the rest of the day. Watched TV in evening.

Sun 24 June

Went to Seasalter to see Mum & Dad. Pam and Maurice came & Auntie Kath and James – quite a nice day – went swimming. Read 'One pair of Hands' by Monica Dickens.

Monica Dickens was the great-granddaughter of Charles Dickens. 'One Pair of Hands' is a memoir describing her exploits as a cook for the upper classes. She went on to write over thirty books – possibly more than her famous great-grandfather.

Sun 29 July

Went to I.O.W. Fred had puncture on the way – arrived at Lymington in time for ferry at 5.30. Was miserable in the evening & wished I hadn't come. Got over it.

I.O.W = Isle of Wight.

Mon 30 July

Was very cold in bed last night. Went for ride in the morning & went to Black Gang Chine. It was very nice. Went to a dance in the evening & had a smashing time. Had awful storm in evening, put all the lights out in Sandown.

Black Gang Chine is the oldest amusement park in the UK. A chine is a ravine – this one was carved from soft rock and has been destroyed by continuous landslides. The park is still a major tourist attraction, but some features have had to be moved inland as erosion continues.

MON 1 OCTOBER

They did some of decorations at work over weekend – made my new room – I bet it will be lovely & did all the plastering on walls & soundproofed the door.

TUES 2 OCTOBER

Went to bookkeeping in evening – it is getting jolly difficult now. Fred met me outside and took me home. Mum was out of course no dinner for me.

FRI 5 OCTOBER

Went to night school – arrived late and left early. Neither Shirley or I have any material yet. Fred met me and brought me home and Roy met Shirley – they make a nice pair.

SAT 6 OCTOBER

Went to pictures with Fred in evening – good film – Fred had an awful headache when he left. Poor darling he often gets these rotten headaches.

Sun 7 October

Fred came over early this afternoon – caught me not ready nothing unusual in that & he told me he went to Town Hall after he left yesterday & stood drinking for a couple of hours. That made me cross. Watched TV in evening.

Mon 8 October

Fred came over about 7.30pm and we went to a political meeting. The speaker was Sir Hartley Shawcross. It was very good but had row with Fred later on – mostly about last Saturday night.

Sir Hartley Shawcross was Labour MP who, at the time, was President of the Board of Trade. The Board of Trade is a government body that advises the government on matters concerning trade commerce and industry.

At the time, Labour were in power but had won the election in 1950 with a slim majority. They called a snap election in October 1951 in the hope of increasing their majority. They lost to the Conservative party, who gained a seventeen seat lead.

According to Eve

OCTOBER

MON 8 — Moon First Quarter
Fred came over about 7.30 & we went to a political meeting. The speaker was Sir Hartley Shawcross. It was very good but had row with Fred later on — mostly about last Sat night.

TUE 9 — Went to book keeping in evening & found that the new chap in class was her — Pat Greer's brother-in-law. Fred wasn't there to meet me, I expect he couldn't make it.

WED 10 — Stayed in in evening — Fred didn't come over — I expect he is working overtime again. Wore my new grey skirt & jacket today — everyone likes it very much.

THU 11 — Stayed in again this evening & again Fred didn't come — I am getting worried as he has been a bit off colour lately or else he has been losing interest in me — which I hope isn't the case.

Tues 9 October

Went to book-keeping in evening and found the new chap in class was here – Pat Green's brother in law. Fred wasn't there to meet me. I expect he couldn't make it.

Weds 10 October

Stayed in in the evening. Fred didn't come over. I expect he is working overtime again. Wore my new grey skirt and jacket today. Everyone liked it very much.

Thurs 11 October

Stayed in again this evening and again Fred didn't come. I am getting worried as he has been a bit off colour recently or else he has been losing interest in me which I hope isn't the case.

Fri 12 October

Met Shirley from work and as we had no material decided not to go to night school but went and had a meal instead. Walked back to Art School where Roy met Shirley. No Fred again. I wish he would come. Aunt Jess came down today.

Sat 13 October

Dorothy's 21st birthday. Party was a great success but I didn't enjoy it because Fred didn't come. Maurice saw him this morning. Met Alan! Got a date for Wednesday.

According to Eve

Dorothy's twenty first birthday party. I think Eve is hidden to the right of Pam and Maurice, who are behind the boy at the front..

According to Eve

Allan, who Eve met at Dorothy's 21st birthday party.

Sun 14 October

Spent nearly all day looking out of the window in case Fred came. Spent all evening sitting in armchair crying my eyes out. I think I have had it. What shall I do? I am certainly not going up for him!

Mon 15 October

Went to work as usual. Am working in waiting room – what fun. Stayed in in evening & set Mum's hair. Then played cards with her and Auntie Jess.

Tues 16 October

Left my book-keeping books at work – silly clot – so caught bus home and stayed in in evening. I played cards with Mum, Auntie and Pam. Played cribbage I won three games and went to bed early.

Cribbage is a card game that uses a peg board to keep track of scores.

Weds 17 October

Work as usual. Went to Paget Hall to dance with Allan. Had a lovely evening he is jolly good fun. Saw Doreen and John there. That will give them something to gossip about.

Paget Hall in Paget Row, Gillingham was another popular dance hall that hosted well known acts and provided ballroom dance lessons. It too has given way to a block of flats now.

Thurs 18 October

Went to meeting with Dad to hear Mr Atlee but we couldn't get in. We heard a bit through the door but couldn't see him so we waited by his car to see him and got a jolly good view.

Clement Attlee was Prime Minister from 1945. When he was elected, a landslide victory made it the first time a labour government had won a majority in Parliament. He had the task of helping Great Britain recover from World War Two. He introduced sweeping reforms including extending The Welfare State, introducing The National Health service and nationalising many industries. Historians consider his government to be one of the most successful.

His tenure ended on 26 October, only a week after Eve tried to hear him speak.

Fri 19 October

Met Shirley from work and as neither of us has got material again we didn't go but went and had a meal – walked back into Rochester. Alan gave me a lift to the fire station I then caught the bus home.

Sat 20 October

Took Carol out in P.M + Allan came over in evening & we went to a dance at gymnasium. Had a marvellous time and we walked home after dance. Allan is very nice and dances quite well.

Sun 21 October

Shocking day today. Fred came over in morning and Allan in p.m. We went for a walk and I had to explain that I couldn't see him again. Went to pictures in evening to see 'Rich, Young and Pretty' with Fred.

'Rich, Young and Pretty' was an American musical comedy about a father who takes his daughter to Paris and tries to prevent his daughter marrying a French man so that she doesn't make the same mistake he made twenty five years earlier.

MON 22 OCTOBER

Still working in waiting room but I shall have to move tomorrow. JR came back today – as handsome as ever.

WEDS 7 NOVEMBER

Work as usual.

THURS 15 NOVEMBER

Work as usual. Went to flicks in evening with Fred & saw 'He ran all the way'. It was quite good.

'He Ran all the Way' was an American crime drama about a heist that goes wrong.

FRI 16 NOVEMBER

Met Shirley from work – she gave her notice in today. We didn't go to night school – we aren't going any more we haven't got the courage to return after so long.

SAT 17 NOVEMBER

Fred came over in morning. In afternoon I took Carol to have her photo taken. I had mine taken in my taffeta dress. Went to gymnasium in evening with Fred and met Allan. Boy oh boy Fred was jealous but recovered. I like Allan.

Taffeta was a crisp, stiff fabric with a sheen that was popular for formal dresses and wedding gowns.

SUN 18 NOVEMBER

Went to tea at the Wanless's and watched TV in evening. The play was utter tripe. Had a quarrel with Fred in the evening. He wants to get engaged and I'm not sure I do.

The play was an American comedy called 'Apples in Eden'.

MON 19 NOVEMBER

Stayed in evening & did some of the mat but it takes so long to grow – didn't see Fred today.

Rug kits were popular at the time. The kit would contain a stiff canvas, woven in squares to provide a grid. It would be painted so that you could see which colours went where in the pattern, like a 'paint by numbers' set. Also included would be a latch hook, a small tool used to pull short lengths of wool through each tiny square and knot them into place. Ready cut lengths of yarn were also supplied. It was a long, slow job.

TUES 20 NOVEMBER

Night school in evening. Fred met me outside & came home with me – made arrangements for tomorrow evening.

WEDS 21 NOVEMBER

Fred met me from work and we went to see 'Latin Quarter' at the Casino – had a lovely evening but decided not to see Fred for a time.

According to Eve

The Casino was a venue in Rochester that has been used as a skating rink and for wrestling matches, as well as being visited by many top dance bands in the 1950s. It was never actually licensed for gambling, so was never a casino!

Latin Quarter was a 1945 British thriller.

THURS 22 NOVEMBER

Work as usual. Stayed in and did some of my white blouse.

FRI 23 NOVEMBER

Went to Dorothy's staff dance at The Chenil *(?)* Galleries. Saw Allan but decided I didn't like him after all. It was a very nice dance.

SAT 24 NOVEMBER

Took Carol to have her photo taken in p.m. – then went to see Shirley. Went to see 'One Touch of Venus' with Pat and Shirley in evening.

'One Touch of Venus' was an American musical comedy about a statue of Venus that comes to life.

SUN 25 NOVEMBER

Went to concert in evening with Mrs Wilkins & Shirl. Iris was dancing in it – very good show. Cyril Fletcher was star of the show. I miss Fred very much – I don't know what to do.

Cyril Fletcher was a popular comedian and actor. At the time he had a role in the BBC show 'What's My Line?'

Mon 26 November

Work as usual. My new room is finished & I will move in as soon as I get a fire. Stayed in in evening and did some of our mat – it is beginning to look nice, all two inches of it.

Tues 27 November

Work as usual followed by does of night school – went to Franklin Rooms afterwards to Mum & Dad to a social. It was quite fun – last year Fred came. It was run by National Savings people.

The National Savings Movement was a government initiative to finance the deficit of its spending. It raised funds to support the Second World War.

Weds 28 November

I moved into my new room at work today. Stayed in in evening. Did some of the

...probably the mat!

According to Eve

✦✦✦✦✦

There are no entries in Eve's diary from here until mid December, but it worth mentioning a terrible tragedy that occurred in the Medway towns on the evening of the fourth of December. I know it deeply affected Fred who told his son about it.

A company of Royal Marine cadets, aged between nine and thirteen, were marching three abreast from one barracks to another, to attend a boxing tournament. They were just past the gates of Chatham Dockyard when a bus approached them at a dark spot where a street lamp had failed. The Officer supervising them ushered them towards the kerb as far as possible, expecting the bus to move around them.

The bus driver did not see them and is reported to have said that he only knew he had hit something 'when the bus started to wobble.' Twenty four boys were killed, and eighteen injured. A public enquiry led to improved street lighting, and new rules about marching convoys carrying lights.

This shocking event was the greatest loss of life due to a road accident in British history and has only been surpassed by one other coach crash since. I imagine that most families would have known someone grieving for a lost son. A memorial parade still happens annually.

✦✦✦✦✦

According to Eve

Fri 14 December

Shirley permed my hair in evening with cold perm. She stayed the night.

Sat 15 December

My hair is awfully frizzy & it sure has taken. Stayed in all evening but Fred didn't come. Perhaps he had to work. Permed Pam's hair today,

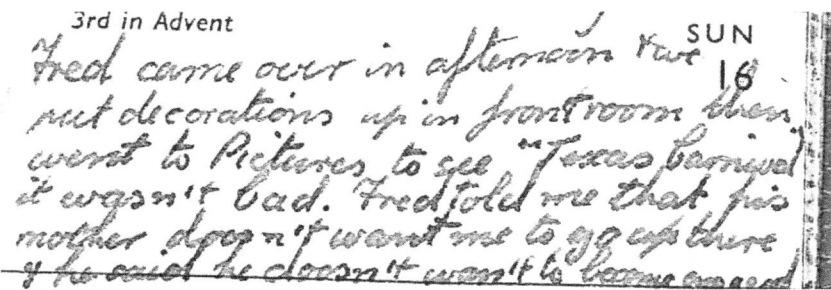

Sun 16 December

Fred came over in afternoon & we put decorations up in front room then went to pictures to see 'Texas Carnival'. It wasn't bad. Fred told me that his mother doesn't want me to go there & he said he doesn't want to become engaged.

Texas Carnival was an American musical comedy.

Mon 17 December

Had awful headache all day. Stayed in evening & went to bed at 9 O'clock. Fred brought the Xmas tree over for me. It's a beauty.

According to Eve

TUES 18 DECEMBER

Missed the 5.45 and caught the 6.23 so was late for night school but we didn't do much work. Fred met me & came over with me. He said he

...and Eve didn't finish the sentence. Could she not bring herself to write what Fred had said? We'll never know.

1952

TUES 1 JANUARY

Work as usual. Fred met me at station & said he was sorry he hadn't been able to come to Auntie Cath's last night.

THURS 3 JANUARY

Work as usual. Went to see the film 'Robin Hood' with Fred and afterwards Fred slapped my face so I slapped his & he walked out on me.

Fred's son was shocked to read this. He had never known his father to be violent.

FRI 4 JANUARY

Went to Cooks to see about our holiday. Will talk it over weekend. No Fred today.

Probably this refers to Thomas Cook & Son, a well known travel company who had branches in most High Streets.

SAT 5 JANUARY

Went out shopping with Mum in p.m. Worked on cakes with CDR in a.m. Mum brought a new coat and lent me the money for a costume. I can pay her back after my holiday.

SUN 6 JANUARY

Stayed in all day. Played cards in evening with Mum &Dad. Went to bed early.

According to Eve

Mon 7 January

Work as usual. Can't make the clients a/c balance. Got rotten cold. Stayed in in evening. Went to bed with hot lemon early.

Tues 8 January

Went to Dr with my cold – then went to work. Stayed in in evening. Didn't go to night school.

Weds 9 January

Stayed at home today with my cold. Did a lot of Mrs Wayman's pullover.

Thurs 10 January

Mum got yard & ¼ of white & yellow material today. I made the yellow blouse in the evening. Very pleased with it.

Fri 11 January

Mrs J wants a white blouse for 15/- & Pat wants a white one with ¾ sleeves for £1. Stayed in in evening.

The currency at the time was pounds, shillings and pence. In the UK we still have pounds. There were twenty shillings to the pound, and twelve pence to each shilling, making it a quite complicated system. Now we have one hundred pence to the pound. 15/- is fifteen shillings, which would be 75p now.

According to Eve

Sat 12 January

Took Carol out in afternoon. Washed hair in evening then went to Joyce's & watched TV. Frankie Howerd – he's very funny.

Frankie Howerd was a very popular comedic actor. He went on to have several hit shows and star in many films including the 'Carry On' series. His catch phrase was 'Titter ye not!'

Sun 13 January

Stayed in all day. Didn't eat any dinner. Set Mum's hair in afternoon – then started Pat's blouse – white with ¾ sleeves. Turned up Mum's coat for her in evening.

Mon 14 January

Sent savings book in. Finished Mum's coat & read 'The Angry Mountain" Very good book, one of Pam's book club books. Mum has made a lovely cake for my birthday.

The Book Club was a subscription organisation that made books affordable and helped promote reading and literature. Often they printed their own editions. Members received a carefully chosen book each month and were encouraged to discuss it with the community.

'The Angry Mountain' was a thriller by British author Hammond Innes

Tues 15 January

Mum spent day in London & bought herself two dresses. Met her for lunch & went straight to night school in evening.

According to Eve

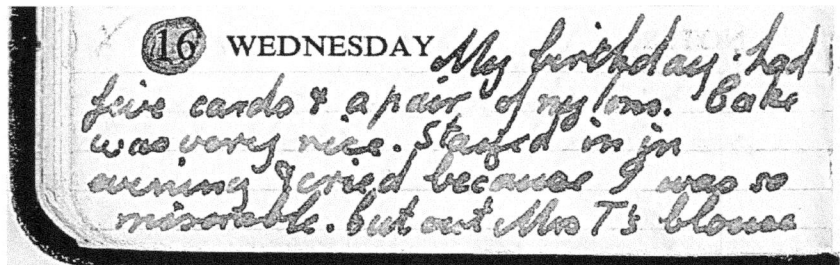

WEDS 16 JANUARY

My birthday. Had five cards & a pair of nylons. Cake was very nice. Stayed in in evening. I cried because I was miserable. Cut out Mrs T's blouse.

THURS 17 JANUARY

Stayed in for a change. Didn't do much at all, just listened to wireless etc. Went to bed early.

FRI 18 JANUARY

Did same as yesterday. Had an awful headache. Didn't go round to Cooks today. Received PO book back.

SAT 19 JANUARY

Bought mauve and yellow material today. Went to flicks in evening with Peggy to see 'Blue Veil'. It was very good.

'The Blue Veil' was an American historical drama starring Jane Wyman.

SUN 20 JANUARY

No sign of Fred. Stayed in all day and evening. Finished Pat's white blouse – it looks very nice.

Mon 21 January

Pat was pleased with blouse. Paid £5 each deposit on holiday. Stayed in in evening. Am very miserable. Washed my hair.

Tues 22 January

Work as usual then night school in evening. No Fred to meet me. I am very upset. Don't know what to do.

Weds 23 January

Work as usual. Books still won't balance. Stayed in in evening. Finished Mrs T's blouse. No Fred again.

Thurs 24 January

Stayed in again this evening for a change. Didn't do anything in particular. It is three weeks today since I last saw Fred.

Fri 25 January

Went with Pam, Peggy & Cynthia to see 'Cinderella' it was very good. Peggy wants to come on holiday with Joan and I.

Sat 26 January

Took Carol out in p.m. Saw Audrey Wanless in High Street. She passed by without speaking. Stayed in in evening – did mauve blouse.

Sun 27 January

Started Cynthia's blouse in morning. Went down to Peggy's at tea-time & we went to the pictures together. Saw 'Encore' it was very good.

'Encore' was an anthology of three W Somerset Maugham's short stories. Maugham introduced each one from his garden in the French Riviera, which no doubt appealed to Eve.

MON 28 JANUARY

Stayed in, no Fred again. Train was late in evening. Didn't do much. Meant to wash my hair but didn't. Read some old 'Women's Owns'.

'Women's Own' was a weekly magazine that had articles on many topics, such as true life stories, recipes, fashion and beauty.

TUES 29 JANUARY

Work as usual then night school. Had 7/10 for my homework. When I got in Dad told me that Tourist Allowance was reduced to £25 = Looks as if I've had my holiday as well.

In 1952, the UK government introduced a Tourist Allowance, which limited the amount of foreign currency individuals were allowed to take on holiday. It was initially set at £100, but due to economic and financial pressure it was reduced to £50 and then £25. This stayed in place until 1966, when it rose to £50.

The average weekly wage for a female clerical worker at the time was between £4 and £7. Given that Eve was just 20, she was earning at the lower end - £4.50, which is equivalent to around £177 now. I know this because there are some faint calculations at the back of one of the diaries where she is estimating how she can save up for her holiday. Payment for making items of clothing features in the reckoning.

Weds 30 January

Work as usual then stayed in in evening; did some of my mat. It is looking very nice.

Thurs 31 January

One month since I saw Fred! Stayed in all evening to see if he would come over at all – he didn't. Did some more of the mat.

Fri 1 February

Payday! Stayed in in evening and listened to wireless. Didn't do anything in particular.

Sat 2 February

Went out in afternoon – saw Audrey again she ignored me. Work in a.m. Stayed in in evening.

Sun 3 February.

Doreen and John came round this morning. I wore my new costume in afternoon & went to Shirleys but she wasn't in. Went home & stayed in for rest of day.

Mon 4 February

Joan & I went round to Cooks today & we have booked to go to Nice for a fortnight. Did my homework in the evening. Still no word from Fred.

Tues 5 February

Work as usual then night school as usual. When I got home I found Shirley was there she had forgotten that I go to night school on Tuesdays. She didn't stay long. Sent Fred a birthday card.

WEDS 6 FEBRUARY

Fred's birthday. The King passed away in his sleep this morning – very unexpected. Wrote to Arthur in evening. I hope Fred had a happy birthday.

King George VI, a well-liked monarch, was fifty six when he died in his sleep at Sandringham. He had had an operation for lung cancer the previous year and never fully recovered, continuing to battle with cancer. It was later reported that a blood clot had stopped his heart. At the time, his daughter Princess Elizabeth, who became queen, was in Kenya, as part of a tour of the commonwealth. She was twenty five. Her coronation did not take place until 1953.

THURS 7 FEBRUARY

Work as usual – Shirley came over in evening & we sat and talked all evening. She said she saw Fred last Tuesday and he had passed his medical A1 and was going into the Merchant Navy.

FRI 8 FEBRUARY

Went straight from train to Shirley's house & spent evening there & Roy & Ron came up with their coaches. Roy and Shirley make a good pair.

SAT 9 FEBRUARY

Got my glasses in morning. Looked after Carol in afternoon. Set Pam's hair in evening, then wrote a letter to Fred. I don't know if I will post it.

According to Eve

Sun 10 February

Went round to Pams for her birthday party today, we played PIT all evening. Took Doreen her present today, some handkerchiefs, she liked them.

PIT was a fast paced board game, originating from America.

Mon 11 February

Work as usual. Stayed in in evening & started putting my snaps in an album. Didn't get very far as I ran out of corners. Posted Freds letter this morning.

Tues 12 February

Caught 5.45 home tonight. It didn't get in until nearly seven so I was late for night school. No Fred to meet me again and no letter when I got home.

Weds 13 February

Stayed in in evening – did some of my mat – bought Shirley's transfers today. I thought she might come over this evening but she didn't.

The transfers were probably temporary tattoos, used for fun. They didn't last long. The design was on a paper backing. Once it was wet, the design could be slid onto the skin.

Thurs 14 February

Had a Valentine card – I hope it is from Fred in answer to my letter. Had letter from Arthur. He has had an accident and may be crippled for life. I do hope he isn't.

According to Eve

Fri 15 February

Had day off today for King's funeral but went into office to watch the procession pass – it was very impressive. Went to Chatham Empire in evening to see Frankie Howerd – very good.

The procession of King George VI was the first funeral of a monarch to be shown on television. It is thought that this occasion led to a steep rise in sales for televisions – although Eve preferred to see it firsthand.

The Empire Theatre was in Chatham High Street on the site by the river where Anchorage House now stands. It closed in 1960.

Sat 16 February

Went out shopping in morning. Saw ignorant Audrey again! & again she ignored me. Went to the pictures with Peggy and Dot & saw 'The Magic Box' it was quite good.

'The Magic Box' was a biographical drama about William Friese-Greene, who designed one of the earliest cinematic cameras and was obsessional about capturing moving images.

Sun 17 February

Stayed indoors all day – very miserable – washed my hair in evening & then went to bed early. I do wish Fred would come back.

Mon 18 February

Work as usual. Pam had a bilious attack & was at home all day. Stayed in in evening for a change. How can I make Fred want me again?

A bilious attack usually referred to abdominal pain or bile causing vomiting.

TUES 19 FEBRUARY

Work again as usual & then night school in evening. No Fred again to meet me but I won't give up hope until I hear it from his own lips that we are through.

WEDS 20 FEBRUARY

Am so fed up and I don't know what to do. Still no letter from Fred. Stayed indoors in evening, cried my eyes out in bed.

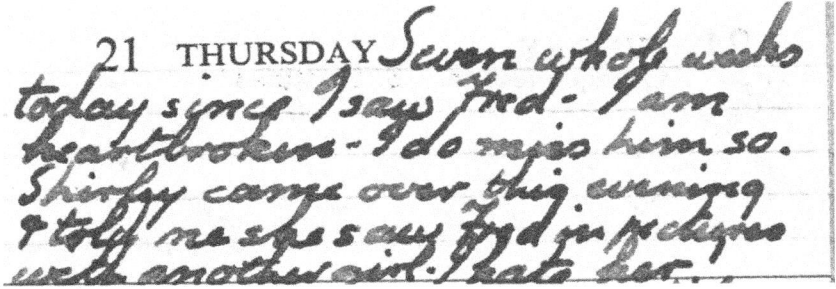

THURS 21 FEBRUARY

Seven whole weeks since I saw Fred – I am heartbroken – I do miss him so. Shirley came over this evening and told me she saw Fred in the pictures with another girl. I hate her!

FRI 22 FEBRUARY

How the weeks do fly – another payday thank goodness. Stayed in in evening – am very sad – went to bed early. Am fed up with everything & everybody.

According to Eve

SAT 23 FEBRUARY

Went out shopping with Mum in morning. I sat by myself in afternoon. Went to pictures with Peggy in evening saw 'The House on the Square' – it was very, very good. Fred went to Pav. With Joan.

This was a different Joan to Eve's friend and work colleague.

'The House on the Square' was a science fiction movie about an atomic scientist who travelled back in time.

Pav was The Pavilion, an imposing dance hall in Canterbury Street, Gillingham. It changed hands several times and was a nightclub before being closed in 2019 and eventually demolished to make way for new flats in 2024.

SUN 24 FEBRUARY

Stayed indoors all day, started Mum's dressing gown. I waited for Fred but he never comes. He went to The Palace with Joan this evening.

Just past the top of Chatham Hill, The Palace was the first 'Super Cinema' to come to the Medway towns, giving tough competition to the smaller picture houses in the High Streets. It was a large, square building with 1,800 plush red seats and had a clock tower that was also used as a fire watch. Over time, it became The Odeon, then a bowling alley. Today it is a camping superstore with forty thousand square feet of showroom.

MON 25 FEBRUARY

Work as usual. Am glad the weekend is over, again. Stayed in in evening. Did my homework for night school.

Tues 26 February

Went to night school tonight it is getting quite difficult & I can't concentrate. No Fred again to meet me.

Weds 27 February

Went to Shirley's in evening. On my way home I saw Keith & Derek & Bill Jarrett. They have all seen Fred with this other girl. Had fish net nylons from Arthur.

Thurs 28 February

Eight long weeks today since I saw Fred. Had rotten cold today. I set Joyce's hair today then went to bed early with hot lemon.

Fri 29 February

Still got rotten cold. Stayed in all evening and started to alter my costume skirt – an awful job. Set my hair before going to bed in case I see Fred tomorrow.

Sat 1 March

Went to Chatham in afternoon – met Dave Silver and Alan Bailie. Went to Pav in evening with Dave then onto Paget. Had a lovely evening – didn't see Fred.

Sun 2 March

Went to Palace to see 'Something to Live For' with Keith Kitchen, met Derek and Brenda afterwards & had coffee. Saw Audrey & she spoke to me! She seemed pleased to see me.

'Something to Live For' was an American drama – it was the first screenplay to mention Alcoholics Anonymous as a way of helping addicts.

MON 3 MARCH

Got rotten cold and nearly lost my voice. Went to Plaza with Steve to see 'Lady Godiva Rides Again'. It wasn't much good. Had a nice evening. Dave is going away for 4 days for RAF exam.

'Lady Godiva Rides Again' was a comedy drama that featured many British stars in cameo roles. It also contains Joan Collins film debut and a small part for Ruth Ellis, who was the last woman in Britain to be executed in 1955. (She shot her lover).

The Plaza was in Duncan Road, Gillingham. In its later days, the building became a film studio – Fraggle Rock and Masterchef were filmed there. When the studio closed, it had a brief spell as Laserquest, before fire damage made the building unsafe. A supermarket is on the plot now.

TUES 4 MARCH

Went to work and then on to night school – my voice is very bad. Went up to Shirleys but she was not in so I left a note for her.

WEDS 5 MARCH

Work as usual. Went to pictures with 'Simmo'. I won't go with him again he's not my type. Saw two very good films.

Thurs 6 March

Nine weeks today. I saw Fred on a bus with the other girl – he winked at me and I wanted to cry. I cried all evening. How long will it take me to get over him? I love him so.

Fri 7 March

Pay day again. Stayed in in the evening and washed my hair & had bath. Meant to go to bed early but didn't.

Sat 8 March

Went to Pav with Dave in evening. Mike Daniels and his Dixielanders – quite good – had a lovely evening. Wrote for local job.

Eve may have meant 'Mike Daniels and his Delta Jazzband' who were a popular Dixieland band at the time.

Sun 9 March

Went to Palace with Dave – saw 'Anne of the Indies' & 'The Small Back Room' – two very good films. Had a nice evening. Dave is good company but not a patch on Fred.

'Anne of the Indies' is loosely based on the life of Anne Bonney, a female pirate.

'The Small Back Room' is about unsung war heroes.

Mon 10 March

Work as usual. Stayed in in evening I did some of Mum's dressing gown.

TUES 11 MARCH

Caught 5.45 home today & saw Joy Hayden. Went to night school – there were only 4 of us there. Came home and listened to light on radio.

The Light Programme was a BBC radio station that broadcast mainstream light entertainment and music. In 1967 it was replaced with Radio 1 and Radio 2.

The Good Companions Club, at the top of Star Hill, Rochester.
Photograph kindly provided by Charles Watson, from the National Heritage List for England at Historic England.
https://historicengland.org.uk/listing/the-list/list-entry/1115706

Weds 12 March

Buses all on strike today at home. Went to Good Companions in evening. Think I will join, it will be something to do in evenings.

Bus drivers were on strike as they were not happy with their working conditions and pay.

Thurs 13 March

Buses are working 'to rule' at home today. Stayed in in evening to wash my hair. Had answer to my letter about local job. I must ring for an interview.

Fri 14 March

Iris's show. Went to see Iris's show with Mum in evening – it was very, very good. I wrote and posted a letter to Fred today. I don't know if I have done rightly or wrongly.

Sat 15 March

Lovely day today. Went out for a ride on dad's cycle this afternoon as buses are out on strike again today. Went to Pav with Dave in evening – had a wonderful time – got home at 1.15am.

> **THE MERCHANT OF VENICE**
> Fri. and Sat. :—
> **TWELFTH NIGHT**
>
> All gangways, corridors, staircases and external passages intended for exit, whether inside or outside the auditorium, shall be kept entirely free from obstruction, whether permanent or temporary, shall not be used as cloakrooms. Safety curtain must be lowered at each performance in view of the audience.
>
> CHATHAM 45471 · Proprietor J. W. EXALL
> **THE PIGGERIES RESTAURANT**
> **CAFE AND SNACK BAR**
> **91 HIGH STREET, CHATHAM**
> Large Hall and Finest Catering for
> Parties, Weddings, Banquets, Receptions, Festivals, etc.
> Open daily 9 a.m.-10.30 p.m. Sundays 12 p.m. to 10.30 p.m.

This image is from a 1954 theatre programme. Thanks to Robert Hall for passing it on after finding it in his research for his book 'Theatre Royal Chatham'.

SUN 16 MARCH

Went to Regent with Dave in afternoon. Afterwards went to Piggeries and have some tea. Met Bill Jarrett & we sat and talked for ages. I got home very late. Mum was annoyed because we stood outside so long.

MON 17 MARCH

Work as usual today – Dave didn't go today so I saw him this evening. We stayed in as he has seen every film being shown locally. Dave is fun to be with but we don't agree on anything.

TUES 18 MARCH

Night school as usual – arrived late as I came in on 5.42 instead of 5.45. Got 9/10 for my homework and essay. I did it by myself for a change it wasn't bad.

Weds 19 March

Work as usual today. Stay in in evening but I couldn't do Mums dressing gown as she wasn't in to try it on.

Thurs 20 March

Stayed indoors in evening and washed my hair. I got it all in waves as Dave likes it instead of curls – I don't know what it will look like.

Fri 21 March

Went to Gaumont Rochester with Peggy to see 'Another Day Tomorrow' & 'Painting the Clouds With Sunshine' Both very good films.

The Gaumont was the new name for The Palace. It had been renamed at the end of 1950.

' Tomorrow is another Day' was a crime drama about an ex-convict who wrongly believes he has killed a man.

'Painting the Clouds with Sunshine' was a lightweight technicolour musical about three Las Vagas theatrical girls looking for husbands.

Sat 22 March

11.30am interview. Don't know if I've got the job or not. They want a reference from B&R's. Saw Dave in afternoon. Bought mauve sweater. Went to Pav in evening – Cyril Stapleton. Had a good time.

B&R's was the solicitors Eve had been working for in London.

Cyril Stapleton was a well known violinist and bandleader. He made several records with EMI and played with many great artists including Frank Sinatra and Matt Monro. He had two chart hits in the United States. You can still hear his music on YouTube.

SUN 23 MARCH

Went to pictures in late afternoon with Dave to see 'The Big Trees' – not very good. Had a meal afterwards then went home. Had a nice day. Doreen and John got engaged today.

Starring Kirk Douglas, The Big Trees is described as a 'lumberjack western.'

MON 24 MARCH

Dave came over about 8.30pm – too late to go anywhere so we stayed in and played cards – he went about 11.30. Dave gets on alright with Mum & Dad thank goodness.

TUES 25 MARCH

Night school tonight – I was late again! Walked down with Leo afterwards. He takes his first exam on Thursday.

WEDS 26 MARCH

Got 2 minutes to 8 this morning – very good seeing I didn't get up until 7.45. Stayed in in evening – so did Mum & Dad - quite unusual.

Thurs 27 March

B&R's had letter asking for my reference today. Stayed in in evening & finished Mum's dressing gown – thank goodness. Washed my hair.

Fri 28 March

Pay day thank goodness. Stayed in in evening. Meant to go to bed early but didn't of course! It snowed today.

Sat 29 March

Stayed in all day. Watched boat race on TV in p.m. Went to Pav with Dave in evening. Had a nice time, it was snowing when we came home and Dave put on his cap – I couldn't stop laughing.

Sun 30 March

Dave came over in p.m & we went to the pictures & afterwards went home & played cards with Mum and Dad.

Mon 31 March

Stayed in in evening and washed my hair. Didn't do much all day – went to bed early. Did my homework for tomorrow.

Tues 1 April

Night school – saw Joyce on the train. There were only 3 of us up at night school – we didn't do very much.

Weds 2 April

Stayed in in evening. Took some plans home to do for Wayman. Got 7/6 for doing them.

According to Eve

7/6 = 7 shillings and sixpence.

THURS 3 APRIL

Took more plans home to do this evening – got another 7/6. Shirley and Roy came over for the beginning – Dad wouldn't stop talking!!

FRI 4 APRIL

Came home on 6.06 with Dave. He came over later in evening & we stayed in and played cards – I lost.

SAT 5 APRIL

Took Carol out in P.M. – met Dave in Chatham & went to Pav in evening with him – 'Saints Jazz Band'. They were quite good. Audrey and Fred's girlfriend Joan were there.

'The Saints Jazz Band' were a successful group who began working with Parlaphone in 1952. They made several 78s. LPs and EPs, supervised by George Martin, who later became famous for his work with The Beatles.

An LP was a 'long player' record, typically having at least seven tracks on each side. An EP was an 'extended play' record, which would have two or three tracks on each side.

Early vinyl records were recorded to be played at 78 rpm (revolutions per minute). The slower a record plays, the longer it plays, but in the early days of recording, slow speeds meant poor sound quality. As technology developed to improve sound, the industry switched to slower speeds – 33rpm for albums (LPs) and 45rpm singles, which only had one track per side.

Sun 6 April

Dave came over in P.M. & we went to Palace to see Jerry Lewis and Dean Martin in 'Sailor Beware' went to 'Franks' afterwards then home.

'Sailor Beware' was a British comedy that gave Michael Caine his first role – albeit a small one.

Mon 7 April

I joined Good Companions in the evening and Dave came with me. I couldn't make him go home. He goes in R.E's tomorrow.

R.E = Royal Engineers

Tues 8 April

No night school tonight went up to Shirleys but she was out. Borrowed her black dress for the fancy dress ball on Easter Monday. Dave went in to the army today.

Weds 9 April

Went to GC's tonight. Met Stella and have played table tennis with Pete & Pete. Left about 10pm. Stella had a bus to catch.

GC = Good Companions club.

Thurs 10 April

Had a surprise – Dave came home on leave – we went to Paget in evening – saw Malcolm there. Had a lovely evening but had row with Dave. He wouldn't go home.

Fri 11 April

Sat in garden all day & started to sew the things on for the fancy dress. Didn't see Dave – still why worry?

Sat 12 April

Went to Chatham in p.m with Carol & lost my purse on the bus. Borrowed 5/6 off Jess. Went up club in evening – saw Charlie and Reg. Reg walked home with me.

Sun 13 April

Played tennis in a.m then went back to club for a drink. Stayed at home in p.m. & went to club in evening. Charlie was there again – he plays wonderfully.

Mon 14 April

The fancy dress dance and ball was terrific & I came 2nd for originality. Met Allan. He is 23 & married but getting a divorce. Really was a wonderful day. Went to Cobham in p.m. with P&M

I think this must be a different Allan to the one she stopped seeing when she got back together with Fred the previous October.

Tues 15 April

Back to work today. Malc came over in evening to see if he could play tennis on Sun. Went up club and saw Allan & Stella. Played table tennis.

Weds 16 April

Went to G.C's in evening with Allan – danced all evening – quite good fun. We walked to Town Hall after.

Thurs 17 April

Stayed in this evening and washed my hair. Went to bed early because I have had a lot of late nights recently. Unpicked the things off Shirley's dress.

Fri 18 April

Stayed in town this evening & went to see 'The Love of Four Colonels' with Peggy. Peter Ustinov was terrific – had lovely time – it was a very funny play.

Peter Ustinov also wrote this play, described as an adult fairy tale. It was performed in London's West End 816 times before transferring to Broadway.

Sat 19 April

Did some plans for M.W. in morning – saw Malc in p.m. who said he would do the others for me. Went to a Primrose Day dance at Town Hall with Allan – had lovely time but he is too serious.

Primrose Day marked the anniversary of the death of the British statesman and prime minister Benjamin Disraeli on 19 April 1881. He had a close friendship with Queen Victoria, who sent a wreath of Primroses to his funeral with a note saying, 'his favourite flower'.

Sun 20 April

Played tennis with Malc in morning and went to his house for coffee afterwards – his parents are very nice. Went to see club show in afternoon & met Malc in evening – he did the plans beautifully.

According to Eve

Mon 21 April

Malcolm came over this evening and sat gassing till nearly 9pm then went up to club but Stella & Allan had gone to my house to see where I'd got to – never mind.

Tues 22 April

Only 4 of us at night school tonight. Got the internal exam next week – oh dear! Must do some swotting before then.

Weds 23 April

Went to GC's in evening. Stella wasn't there but Allan was – he came home with me. His divorce comes up next Tuesday.

Thurs 24 April

Stayed in tonight washed my hair & Mums hair & had bath. Did some ironing & packed my week-end case. Was very late to bed.

Fri 25 April

Pay day – hoorah! Went home from office with Joan for weekend. Mrs H took us for a drive in evening till it got dark.

This Joan was a work colleague, not Fred's new girlfriend

Sat 26 April

Went round Enfield with Joan in morning then we went to the races at Enfield Chase. Sat on top of the car & had a wonderful view; had very nice time.

This would have been Northaw Races, who have been home to point to point horse racing since the 1930s.

According to Eve

Sun 27 April

Sat in garden all afternoon & then walked to their golf club to meet Mr & Mrs H. Went for a drive in evening – enjoyed it very much. How the weekends do fly.

Mon 28 April

Went straight to office from Joans in morning. Went to G.C's in evening & Alan came home with me & caught the train home. Stella was up there this evening. Dad said I can learn to ride his bike.

Tues 29 April

Night school tonight. Alan met me after & the divorce went off alright today. He came home with me and left about 10pm.

Weds 30 April

Stayed in in evening. Shirley and Roy came over + so did Malcolm we looked through a lot of old photos. Malc is very good fun.

Thurs 1 May

Malcom came over again this evening – we just sat talking. He has booked up for tennis on Sunday: will see him then.

Fri 2 May.

Went up the club this evening – saw Allan – he didn't come home with me thank goodness! We danced most of the evening.

According to Eve

Sat 3 May

Tennis season opened today – played in p.m. + went to dance in club in the evening with Alan. Had a minor row on the bus coming home – never mind.

Sun 4 May

Played tennis in the rain with Malc this morning. Stayed in for the rest of the day & cut Joan's dress out. Malc said he might come over but of course he didn't.

Mon 5 May

Went up the club in evening – didn't do very much. Watched the variety section rehearsing for a time. Left the club late so that Allan couldn't come home with me.

Tues 6 May

Night school this evening. They closed the canteen so I was starving. Was furious because Alan met me & was horrible to him – so didn't come home with me.

Weds 7 May

Stayed in this evening & did some studying for exam next Friday. Went to bed early for a change – did a little of Joan's dress.

Thurs 8 May

Finished Joan's dress this evening. Malcolm came over for a very little while then did some studying.

Fri 9 May

Caught 5.21 home tonight. Had a meal at GC's then went for the internal exam. I didn't find it terribly difficult. Liz walked out after 1 hour.

Sat 10 May

Played tennis all afternoon. Allan was there & I went to Central with him in the evening. Had very nice time but packed him up today - he isn't half as nice as F.

The Central Hotel on Watling Street was a large, Tudor style public house with a large function room and car park. Originally a 'road house', coaches would stop here on their way to the coast. It was converted to a night club and eventually demolished in the mid 80s.

Sun 11 May

Played tennis with Malc in morning – then it rained. I stayed indoors for the rest of the day. I wish Fred would come back to me.

Mon 12 May

My last day of B & R's. M's clerk took over today. Stayed in town with Peggy in evening & saw Michael Redgrave, Googie Withers & Sam Wanamaker in Winter Journey it was very, very good.

This play, at St James's Theatre, London had opened the previous month. It is described as a moving drama about a self-destructive alcoholic actor and his long-suffering wife.

According to Eve

Tues 13 May

Started my new job today. I think I will be A OK. Went to night school in evening and Mr Price said we all passed our county exam – thank goodness. Came home by myself.

Weds 14 May

Took Malc up to play tennis with the club this evening & saw Yvonne up there. She has gone back with Derek Armitage. She seems very happy.

I assume this is the same Yvonne that was engaged to Arthur earlier but can't be sure.

Thurs 15 May

Work as usual. Am settling in a bit now. Stayed in for the evening & washed my hair. Played the piano and went to bed early. How I miss Fred.

Fri 16 May

 Pay day today! Shirley and Roy came over in evening & Malc said he was coming too but he didn't. Nobody likes me & I only like one person and that of course is Fred.

Sat 17 May

Played tennis all afternoon – Larry came up. Went to dance at club in evening & met Geoff. Had quite a pleasant day. Bought Mum's present today.

Sun 18 May

Went to Margate with Roy and Shirley today. Had lovely time if only Fred had been with me it would have been perfect.

Mon 19 May

Played tennis with club in the evening. Yvonne was there. Went up club after & met Geoff & Larry was there too.

Tues 20 May

Night school. I got 81% for my county exam & came top. There was only Leo and myself there tonight.

Weds 21 May

Geoff took me out for lunch today. I went out to Jess's in evening to see about her blouse. Went to bed early.

Thurs 22 May

20 weeks today!

Geoff took me out for a ride this evening, we went to East Farleigh & called in at The Malta on the way back – it didn't seem the same without Fred.

The Malta was a popular riverside inn and restaurant on the outskirts of Maidstone, about twenty minutes' drive away. Reg sang with a band that had a residency there in the 1960's. One night they were playing in the upstairs restaurant and so many people got up to dance that they shook the chandelier off its hook in the bar below! Fortunately no one was hurt.

There have been many changes and extensions over the years, but The Malta is still in business. It is a Beefeater Inn these days.

Fri 23 May

Went to see GC's play at the Globe this evening called 'They Came to a City'. It was very good and well acted. I served coffee in interval so got in for nothing.

'They Came to a City' was a play by J.B. Priestly that imagines a post-war Utopia.

The Globe Theatre was located inside the Royal Marine Barracks in Dock Road, Chatham. It was built in 1879 when the barracks were extended, and was used for lectures, concerts and plays. It was often used by local amateur dramatic societies.

Sat 24 May

Went to see Mr Bowen today & he started to burn out my wart. Started Carol's dress. Went up club – met Geoff then went to gym to a dance. Had quite a nice time. Went to 1st House of the Empire before I went to the club & saw Elsie & Doris Waters. Keith Kitchen had a turn in the show he was quite good.

Sun 25 May

Stayed in in morning. Went to club to tea dance in pm – met Eric Wade up there & went to see 'Five Fingers' with Geoff in the evening it was quite good.

'Five Fingers' was a film noir spy drama, based on a true story from 1943-44.

Mon 26 May

Stayed in in evening & did a bit of swotting for my exam. Played the piano and went to bed early for a change.

TUES 27 MAY

The last class of night school this evening. I left early as Auntie Jenny and Uncle Ernest came to see us. They want to buy a bungalow at Hoo.

Hoo is a village situated on the rural peninsula that separates the River Medway from the River Thames.

WEDS 28 MAY

RSA Exam.

Had a meal at the club then went to Fort Pitt. The exam was shocking – I am sure I haven't passed. Went to club after.

THURS 29 MAY

Eric came over this evening & he came down to Mr Bowen with me. Had my wart cut out – it didn't hurt. Eric stayed late.

FRI 30 MAY

Went up GC's with Eric in evening & we danced. I also danced with Allan & Geoff – quite an old flames party in fact.

SAT 31 MAY

Didn't have to work this morning. I met Aunty Jess in the afternoon & we had a party in the evening for Mum's silver wedding next Weds.

SUN 1 JUNE

Went to tea with Mrs Wade & sat talking to Eric all evening about Fred. What a wonderful subject.

MON 2 JUNE

It was raining today so we couldn't go up the river. Instead we went to see 'That's My Boy' & I saw FRED! I gave him his ring back & he said he will write – he is going to Korea.

'That's My Boy' was a musical comedy film starring Dean Martin and Jerry Lewis

TUES 3 JUNE

Went to GC's with Eric & played table tennis & I went into the Theatre Group. Eric came home with me as he had some things to collect from my house.

WEDS 4 JUNE

Went to Yvonne & Derek's engagement party at Yvonne's house. Alan Bolton was there. Mr Trowell brought me home as it was late.

I assume this is a different Alan to the Allan she 'packed up' with on 10 May, but can't be sure.

THURS 5 JUNE

Played tennis with GC's and Eric came up. He came home with me wot a thrill! I played a good game tonight at tennis.

FRI 6 JUNE

Aunty Jess went home today. I stayed in in evening & did some sewing. Washed my hair.

SAT 7 JUNE

Went to a dance at the Town Hall with Yvonne, Derek & Alan & had a very nice evening. Alan brought me home.

SUN 8 JUNE

Went out to Derek's bungalow to a little party. Wendy got engaged the same time as Yvonne & Derek. Had a nice evening – their bungalow is wonderful.

MON 9 JUNE

At last Dad's Bantam came back & went out on it this evening. I went round to see Doreen & John – they were surprised to see me on it.

Mum remembered the Bantam fondly and always had a love of motorcycling. She was 5'2' and couldn't ride bigger motorbikes unless someone with long legs was riding pillion, because she was too short to hold them upright at traffic lights.

According to Eve

Tues 10 June

Went to see 'With a Song in my Heart' with Alan, Yvonne & Derek. It was quite good. Derek failed his medical for the Navy today.

'With a Song in my Heart' was a biographical musical drama, recounting the true story of Jane Froman, and American actress and singer who was crippled when the plane she was on crashed landed into a river.

Weds 11 June

Went out on Bantam with Doreen & John to the top of Bluebell Hill. Got home just before 10pm.

Thurs 12 June

Stayed in first part of evening & then went out for a ride along the road. Saw Johnny Duffield & stopped & talked to him for quite a while. I got home just before lighting up time.

Fri 13 June

Pay day hooray! Had income tax rebate of 18/-. Went on Bantam to see Shirley & she told me she is getting engaged to Roy. Her ring is awfully sweet.

Sat 14 June

Went to London in morning with Yvonne and Mrs Armitage. Went to dance in Town Hall in evening with Alan. Yvonne & Derek decided to come at the last minute & stayed to tea.

Chatham Town Hall is an imposing renaissance style building that was opened in 1900. It originally housed the local council and had a multipurpose hall with stage above. When councils merged and moved to larger premises, after a few years it became The Brook Theatre. In 2023 it closed temporarily for a major refurbishment.

Chatham Town Hall. Picture courtesy of John Stratford
https://flickr.com/photos/john47kent/3747151975

Sun 15 June

Alan came over in p.m & we went to pictures to see 'The River'. It was quite an unusual film.

Shot in Calcutta, 'The River' is based on a Rumer Godden novel, telling the story of a girls coming of age, using the river as a metaphor.

Mon 16 June

Went out on Bantam with Doreen & John – went on the road to Sheerness & came back the Lower Road way. I lost them but arrived home at the same time.

Sheerness is o seaside town on the Isle of Sheppey, an island near the mouth of the River Medway. It dates back to the sixteenth century, when it was built as a port to protect the river from invasion.

Tues 17 June

Went out to Derek's house and we made a start on the bridesmaid's dresses – they will look very pretty I think when they are done.

Weds 18 June

Got my passport today. Roy & Shirley & Alan came over in evening. Stayed in and talked all evening.

Thurs 19 June

Went out for a ride with Doreen & John to Allington. Didn't get in until quite late. I lost them again. John was very cross.

According to Eve

Allington is a village near Maidstone with an impressive, restored Norman Castle, which is a private residence.

Fri 20 June

Went to the fair with Alan this evening. Made him feel sick by going on the Octopus. Watched the fireworks. They were quite good.

The Octopus is a fairground ride.

Sat 21 June

Work in the morning. Doreen came to dinner & then gave me a home perm – finished about 9 o'clock. It has been ok I think.

Sun 22 June

I went up GC's this afternoon & evening. Alan came up in evening. I had a premonition that Fred was writing to me today. I must be going round the bend.

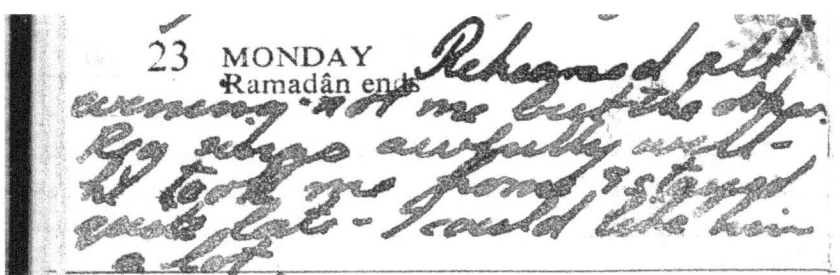

Mon 23 June

 Rehearsal all evening – not me but the others. Reg sings awfully well. He took me home and stopped quite late. I could like him a lot.

According to Eve

TUES 24 JUNE

Went to tennis in evening on my bantam – Larry was there – I played very badly – lost both sets. Never mind.

I love that 'dad's bantam' is now 'my bantam'!

WEDS 25 JUNE

Went up the club with Reg this evening. They rehearsed most of the evening. Reg sang with me. Boy oh boy!

THURS 26 JUNE

Went to top of Bluebell Hill with Doreen & John. Have been in a wonderful mood all day. Called in and saw Reg at lunchtime

Bluebell Hill is a local beauty spot. Part of the North Downs, it is visited for its panoramic views across the Kent countryside. It is still a nature reserve.

FRI 27 JUNE

Reg came up for me and we went to club together. The shows went ok. Reg came home with me and stayed until about 12.30. I have an awful crush on him.

SAT 28 JUNE

Work in a.m. Saw Reg on way to work. Gave Doreen a home perm in p.m.& went to see Reg in p.m as well. Went to dance at Drill Hall in evening with Alan – wasn't bad but too hot for dancing.

Sun 29 June

Played tennis in a.m with Reg & then we went back to Erik & Con's place for supper. Had a very nice time the weather is terrific.

The Good Companions tennis team. Reg is on the left in the front row, Eve is next to him.

Mon 30 June

Went to club. Sat in garden as it was so hot. Reg came home with me – stayed quite late & Dad got annoyed. Reg is wonderful I think I am falling hard.

According to Eve

Tues 1 July

Went to Grand with Reg this evening to see 'The Strip' with Louis Armstrong in it & it was very good. I keep singing 'A kiss to build a dream on' – it came from this film.

'The Strip' is an American crime film based in the nightclubs of Sunset Strip in Hollywood. You can still hear Louis Armstrong singing this on YouTube.

Weds 2 July

Went to Yvonnes for tea then on to tennis. Yvonne and I went down the club after to meet Reg & I was very surprised to see Fred there – came straight home with Reg.

Thurs 3 July

Stayed in this evening. Reg came up – didn't do anything in particular – just sat talking. Reg is awfully nice. I feel as if I have known him years.

Fri 4 July

Went to Oakwood with Derek, Yvonne & Alan to see Miss Moore – Fred was there. Alan came home with me & I told him I wouldn't be seeing him anymore.

Another Alan bites the dust! Is that the third?

Sat 5 July

Called in to see Reg in p.m. Bought new dress & sandals. Fred came over at teatime but he didn't stay long. Went up GCs with Reg in the evening. Watched TV & got home quite late. Quite a day today has been!

Sun 6 July

Fred came over this morning and took me out for a drink. Auntie Jennie and Uncle Eric came to lunch. Shirley came over in p.m. I played tennis with Reg and then we went down the club. Reg MC'd the Sunday Serenade.

Mon 7 July

Went up GC's with Reg this evening. They were rehearsing for the Variety Group Dance. I got told off by Dad for keeping Reg too late.

Tues 8 July

Went with Reg to see a chap called Ernie Bucket – he runs a lot of shows – we listened to some records of the Truculent concert. Very enjoyable evening.

HMS Truculent was a submarine that tragically sank following a collision, killing sixty four men. It had just been refitted at Chatham Dockyard. Many employees of the dockyard were on board at the time for post refit checks. There is still an annual memorial service in Chatham.

Weds 9 July

Met Yvonne & played tennis – played quite well then went to club to meet Reg. Dad went to Oxford today. Sent money for my holiday to Joan.

Thurs 10 July

Had letter from Joan this morning. Reg played in match tonight on Ebenezer Court & I played on open. Called in for a drink on the way home. Reg stayed quite late.

Fri 11 July

Joan came to stay this weekend & we went up the club and she met Reg. Joan hasn't been very well. We are both very excited about the holiday. She brought our tickets today, all well I hope.

Sat 12 July

Had to work in a.m & Shirley permed Jessies hair in p.m. Went up club in evening & saw Reg. Reg came home with me and we stayed up very late talking.

Bought 'Daybreak' by Anthony Gibbs from Lewises.

Anthony Gibbs was the son of Sir Philip Armande Gibbs, who was one of nine siblings. Five of them became writers.

'Daybreak' was published in 1950.

Sun 13 July

Joan & I stayed in bed all morning. Pam and Maurice came to tea & we played Newmarket in the evening. I lost 1/7½ - ruin. We went to bed quite early. Didn't see Reg today.

Newmarket was a card game based on horse racing. Players bet on their horse and lost their money if their horse lost. My grandmother played it with us when we were children. She liked any game that had an element of gambling.

Mon 14 July

Went to GC's this evening with Reg they were rehearsing for the dance next Sat nearly all evening. Reg stayed til 12.15 & Mum was very annoyed.

Tues 15 July

Went out to Walderslade this evening. Fred came too – he stayed talking to me until 12.15 – he wants me to go back with him. I am doubtful – I couldn't trust him.

Weds 16 July

Fred came over for a little while & took me up to tennis. Played with Reg & then went down the club with him – don't feel too well today.

Thurs 17 July

Altered my sun dress & did other odd jobs, then met Reg from tennis – had a drink on the way home & Reg stayed quite late. I won't see him again until after my holiday.

Fri 18 July

Went out to lunch with Murtle today & stayed in in evening. Finished my packing – I had a bath and went to bed early. I am so excited but have an awful cold.

Sat 19 July

Mum & Dad saw me off today. I met Joan at Victoria & we are now well on our way. Have very nice travelling companions & the train isn't too uncomfortable.

Victoria is the train station in London where trains left for the coast. From there. Eve took a ferry across the channel, then another train to Nice, which took over eleven hours.

Sun 20 July

Eventually arrived at Nice – very tired & very dirty – had dinner at hotel which is very nice then went for a stroll but went to bed quite early as we were tired.

Thurs 24 July

Went swimming all day today & went to Le Verdun and then on to The Folies – a night club – had a wonderful time – there were 17 of us.

Fri 25 July

Went swimming in morning & went to the village in p.m. with a chap from the hotel called Victor Porter. It was a very nice place. Went out with Bill & May in evening.

Sat 26 July

Went on coach trip to St Paul, Grasse, Gourdon, St Cezaire & Pont du Loup etc – very nice. Met 3 horrible chaps at Le Verdun tonight. Joan and I quickly came back to the hotel.

Grasse is the centre of France's perfume industry.

Sun 27 July

Went swimming in morning for last time – went to sleep in p.m. I went for a drink in evening with May & Bill & the Shepherds.

Mon 28 July

Sat on beach today. Met John & Graham in the evening in their MG. We went dancing & then John & I rode in the dicky seat – great fun.

A dicky or rumble seat was an upholstered seat that folded out from the back, where the boot would usually be, in sports cars.

TUES 29 JULY

Went on coach trip to San Remo today and went dancing with John and Graham took Joan to Monte Carlo for the evening. Had a very pleasant day.

San Remo is a coastal medieval town about 34 miles from Nice, over the border in Italy.

WEDS 30 JULY

Went on beach with the crowd in a.m – none of us swam, Joan went in in p.m. & I sunbathed. Went out with crowd in evening.

THURS 31 JULY

Bought the rest of presents in a.m. Stan and Lily came to Nice in p.m. Went to the corner for a drink then went to bed early – did some packing.

FRI 1 AUGUST

Had one last walk to the beach today. Left Nice at 12.21 and started the long journey home. Very nice travelling companions.

SAT 2 AUGUST

Arrived indoors just after 5pm – Mum & Dad were pleased to see me. Reg came up in evening & we sat talking then went for a stroll.

Sun 3 August

Went out on bantam this morning – saw Reg up the club. Reg came up in p.m. & we went up the club again. He played the bongos with the guest pianist Reg Adams – wasn't bad.

According to Eve

This is Eve's BSA Bantam, with Reg at the front. He was never a motorbike rider as far as I know.

According to Eve

Mon 4 August Bank Holiday

Went to club on my bantam this morning. Reg came up in p.m. & we went to the flicks then up the club. Stayed up quite late – I have still got it bad.

Tues 5 August

Back to the office. – oh Lord. Reg came up in the evening & we went round to Pams to return Maurice's camera. Reg went about 10.45. I meant to wash my hair but didn't.

Weds 6 August

No tennis today because of weather so hey! I went to club in evening. Watched TV & left about 10pm. I am getting much too fond of Reg!

Thurs 7 August

Went to The Empire with Reg this evening to see 'The Stargazers'. I enjoyed the show very much. I had a drink in Sun Hotel then came home.

The Stargazers were a popular vocal band that had two number one singles and a couple of other chart entries before rock and roll and pop music took over. They recorded with Frank Sinatra and Peggy Lee, also they provided backing on Petula Clark's early recordings.

The Sun Hotel was also in Chatham High Street, very close to The Empire Theatre. Built on the site of a pub that had been destroyed in a fire, it was advertised in 1864 as 'A modern Hotel known to naval officers the world over.' It was demolished around 1966 and has been replaced by offices and an education centre.

Fri 8 August

Went up to Yvonnes tonight & then on to Mrs A's got the material for my dress. Washed my hair & then at 10pm Fred arrived – I told him it was no good so he didn't stay long.

Sat 9 August

Went up club in evening with Reg – sat talking to Doug & Win for most of the evening – played bar billiards with Reg – watched TV then came home.

Sun 10 August

Went up club for tea – no tennis as it was raining. Was dancing all evening – then watched TV.

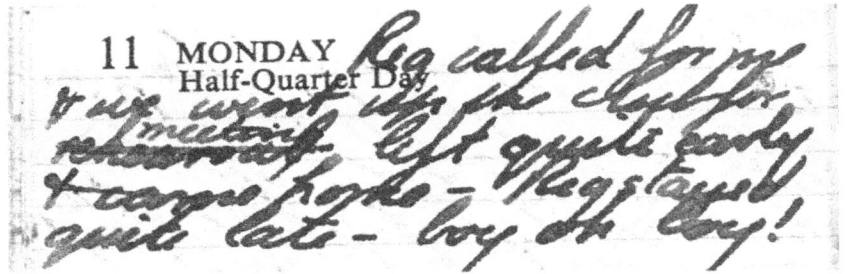

Mon 11 August

Reg called for me & we went up the club for meeting. Left quite early & came home – Reg stayed quite late – boy oh boy!

Tues 12 August

Lovely day today so went up early and played tennis. Reg came up late but didn't play – went down the club for a little while.

According to Eve

Weds 13 August

Went up to club for rehearsal tonight – new show coming up – so there's lots of work to be done. Left quite early.

Thurs 14 August

Went to the picture house with Reg to see 'Sunny Side of the Street' I enjoyed it, it was very good – got home quite early.

The Picture House was next door to The Empire Theatre and had the same owners. It was renamed 'The Empire Cinema' in 1953.

'Sunny Side of the Street' was a musical comedy about an aspiring singer, starring Frankie Laine.

Sat 16 August

Was in office by myself a.m. – permed Peggy's hair in p.m. – just finished & met Reg on his way up for me – went up to the club for a little while.

Sun 17 August

Reg played with match with Jackie in a.m. – he won – we played tennis all p.m. & went down the clamp afterwards. Danced, they played a lot of waltzes. Hey ho!

Mon 18 August

Reg called for me quite early & we went up the club for rehearsal of variety. Left just after 10pm & wouldn't let Reg stay too long because too much pash.

I assume 'pash' is slang for passion!

TUES 19 AUGUST

Stayed in this evening & finished my bridesmaid's dress, it looks very nice. Went to bed quite early. I missed him. Bought wedding present for Yvonne.

WEDS 20 AUGUST

Rehearsal again this evening. Buster, Arthur and I went through the Charlie Chaplin sketch. Reg stayed quite late again.

The Charlie Chaplin sketch. Arthur is playing Charlie Chaplin, so I assume the other man is Buster. Photograph kindly provided by Arthur's daughter, Lynn Armstrong.

According to Eve

THURS 21 AUGUST

Reg and I went to the Park Fete this evening & stayed & watched the fireworks – very good display. Reg came in for a cup of tea but didn't stay very long.

FRI 22 AUGUST

Played my match off against Berny King & lost 6:2. Went home then & washed & set my hair ready for tomorrow. Had lunch out with Murtle today – called in & saw Reg.

SAT 23 AUGUST

Had bath in a.m. Mum & Dad went to Ramsgate. Wedding went off very well – I got a bit tipsy. Came home.

Reg came up & we went to Dot and Ron's wedding reception. Came home about 11.30 & I felt a bit sick – but I wasn't. Reg was so sweet and considerate. Quite a day on the whole.

It sounds as if Eve attended two weddings, as Derek and Yvonne got married on this day.

According to Eve

Derek and Yvonne's wedding. Eve was a bridesmaid, and made the bridesmaids' dresses. Eve is on the right.

Sun 24 August

Went for a ride on the bantam in the morning & called in the club to see Reg. Went up club in p.m. too – did some rehearsing – went down Arthurs & saw his costume – very nice too.

Mon 25 August

Reg called for me and we went up to rehearsal. Our act is coming along OK I think. Reg came home with me & stayed quite late much to Mum's annoyance.

Tue 26 August

Reg came up & we stayed in this evening – I started to make my sari – it looks awful. Reg went home early tonight. That pleased Mum.

Weds 27 August

I went up to play tennis today but there was no one there. I went down the club & saw Reg – didn't stay very late. Charlie played the piano.

Thurs 28 August

Called in at Arthurs for Bill's guitar & then Reg & I went to Eric & Cons for a rehearsal of 'Walking my Baby Back Home' & 'Kiss to Build a Dream On'. – very nice evening.

'Walking my baby Back Home' was a popular song written in the 1930s. Many artists recorded it, but Nat King Cole had a big hit with in 1952.

Fri 29 August

Went up club with Reg & listened to a band recording in the hall – Arthur Mason & his trio -they were corny! Did a bit of rehearsing after – Reg is wonderful but very passionate. Reg said he loves me – wonder if he means it.

I couldn't find any information about Arthur Mason. Maybe Eve was right.

Sat 30 August

Work in a.m. – stayed in in p.m. – had bath & washed my hair. Reg & I went to GC's Mad Hatters dance at Corn Exchange. Had quite a nice time. Reg told me he loves me this evening. Boy oh boy!

I have no idea what the Mad Hatters dance involved, but there is a photo.

Photo provided by Arthur's daughter, Lynn Armstrong.

According to Eve

Sun 31 August

Went up club on my bantam in a.m. – saw Reg – Alan came over after lunch with some photos of wedding – went up to play tennis later then on to club. Larry beat me 6:1. Reg told me he loves me again.

Mon 1 Sept

Went to tea with Myrtle & then on to the club to see Reg. My curtain is at last beginning to look like a sari. Both Reg & I felt very tired tonight.

Tues 2 Sept

Called in & saw Reg lunch time – I stayed in this evening – cut out Mum's coat & did some of my sari – went to bed early. Reg went up Eric & Con's this evening to rehearse.

Weds 3 Sept

Reg met me from the office tonight & came home for tea – we went up GC's for rehearsal of 'Top Hat' everything went wrong. I told Reg I loved him – he is wonderful.

'Top Hat' was a famous 1935 Irving Berlin film starring Fred Astaire, but I suspect that this was a name they gave to a variety show and was not connected to the film.

Thurs 4 Sept

I called in & saw Reg on my way home from the office – didn't see him in evening. We both stayed in for an early night I cut the little boys coat out. Was in bed by 10p.m.

Fri 5 Sept

Reg came up for me & we went up the club. Did nothing in particular – danced for a while then just sat talking with Arthur, Betty etc. Reg stayed quite late this evening.

Sat 6 Sept

Win came over this afternoon & Reg came up in evening & Reg & I went to Yvonne & Dereks for Dereks birthday. Quite a pleasant evening. They all like Reg. As so do I.

Sun 7 Sept

Stayed in in a.m. because of rain. Reg came up in p.m. & we went to pictures to see 'Dumbo' & 'The Wonder Man' – I enjoyed them both – then went up club – had some tea & watched TV. Had a cup of char at Arthurs then came home.

'Dumbo' is Disney's famous 1941 animation about a flying elephant.

'The Wonder Man' could be one of two films. There is a 1920 silent movie with this name, but it seems more likely that Eve watched 'Wonder Man', a 1945 musical starring Danny Kaye.

Mon 8 Sept

Very cold today. Nearly froze in the office. Went up GC's in this evening and met Reg – didn't see much of him all evening till we came home. Rehearsal went better this evening.

Tues 9 Sept

Reg & I & P & M went up to see Dot & Ron. Had a couple of drinks and a piece of their wedding cake – she showed us all their photos. Left just after 11pm. Broke electric fire in the office & all the internal phones.

According to Eve

WEDS 10 SEPT

Reg met me from the office today & we went to tea with his Mum & Dad. They are both very nice – went to the club later with Reg. He stayed quite late.

THURS 11 SEPT

I went straight to Arthur & Betty's place for tea today & Len came down in evening to take photo of Arthur & I in our Indian costumes. Reg called in about 10.45 & took me home. I am crazy about him.

Len was Leonard Hill, a photographer I remember from childhood who took family portraits. For many years he had a studio at 280 High Street, Rochester, where a parade of shops was situated on a bank at a higher level to the road. Houses have been built here since.

Blacking your face to imitate someone from another race isn't something we do today. It is regarded as inappropriate and likely to cause offence by promoting stereotypes or a negative view of another culture. It began centuries ago – as far back as Shakespeare's Othello - and grew in popularity in the USA from 1830. It is a tradition rooted in racism – black people (especially slaves) were mocked for the entertainment of white people, which was demeaning and hurtful.

It began to wane in the 1940's as the Civil Rights movement gained momentum but didn't disappear completely. In fact, the popular BBC show 'The Black and White Minstrels' didn't start until 1958 – six years after Eve's performance – which shows us that it was considered acceptable in Eve's day. An internal memo described the show as "a disgrace and an insult to coloured people" in 1962 but it wasn't removed from its regular spot until 1978.

According to Eve

For their telepathy act, Eve and Arthur dressed up as Indians and appeared to demonstrate mind reading.

Fri 12 Sept

Had my hair set at lunch time – went up club this evening. Reg had a rehearsal on & I was Duty Steward so I just wandered around. Reg stayed late & Mum & Dad got very annoyed.

Sat 13 Sept

Work in a.m. – called in to see Reg p.m. & then went to tea at his house – took Brian up to meet Reg at 7 o'clock. We went up club in evening as Reg hadn't heard from Malc – he was there and told Reg he lost the money for his holiday on the dogs. Poor darling Reg was very disappointed & upset. He does need a holiday & won't go alone.

Sun 14 Sept

Reg came up this p.m & we went to his house for a cup of tea then we went up to London to the Albert Hall to see 'Jazz at the Prom'. Had a lovely day enjoyed it very much.

Jazz became a staple offering at The Royal Albert Hall from 1952 Top of the bill on this day was Vic Lewis and his Orchestra, who went on to release an album of Gerry Mulligan arrangements in 1954.

Mon 15 Sept

Reg phoned this a.m. & we went home on bus to lunch together. I stayed in in evening. Win came over. She bought me a box of chocolates. She decided she doesn't want net under dress now. I missed Reg this evening. I wonder if he missed me?

Tues 16 Sept

Reg met me again lunch time & he came up this evening & we went to see 'Mandy' – it was quite good film but not so sad as thought it would be. Reg didn't stay long this evening.

'Mandy' was a melodrama based on a Novel by Hilda Lewis. It tells the tale of a deaf child and her parents' struggle to come to terms with her condition.

Weds 17 Sept

Reg met me tonight & came home to tea. Pam & Maurice popped in for a few minutes & then we went up the club. There was a rehearsal but it didn't last long!

Thurs 18 Sept

Had a day off today. Reg & I went to London & met Pam & Joan for lunch – looked around shops in p.m. & went to Prince of Wales to see Norman Wisdom in 'Paris to Piccadilly' in evening – wonderful day!

Theatre Impresario Bernard Delfont decided to bring a revue from Folies Bergere in Paris to London. There were 2,000 performances at the Hippodrome before a new edition called 'Paris to Piccadilly' opened at The Prince of Wales theatre.

Fri 19 Sept

Left office a few minutes early tonight – had my tea then went to enrol for night school. The went to a dance at the NAAFI with Reg, Nell & Joe – a very good evening.

According to Eve

NAAFI was the Navy Army and Air Forces Institute – a company formed by the government to provide recreational facilities and sell goods to the British armed forces. They ran many bars, clubs and shops. They are still in existence, but numbers were scaled back after the second world war.

Nell was Reg's cousin. Their mothers were twins and lived a few doors apart.

Sat 20 Sept

Saw Reg on my way home from work – then had lunch & caught 1.54 to Vic & met Alan. We went around the House of Commons & Westminster Abbey – Saw 1st round of 'London Laughs' with Tony Hancock, Jimmy Edwards & Vera Lynn. Was a hilarious show. Had a meal after & caught 10.18 home.

This review was a big hit for the Adelphi Theatre. Excerpts were played on the BBC's Light Service radio.

Sun 21 Sept

Went out for the day with Pete & Pat & Reg. We went to Hastings & the weather was quite good after one heavy shower – came back via Tenterden. Had a lovely day, enjoyed it very much.

Mon 22 Sept

Reg called for me & we went up club for rehearsal. Neither of us felt very well tonight – Reg thinks he has a chill – I dosed him with Veganin.

Veganin tablets are still on the market – they are a mix of Paracetamol, Codeine and Caffeine.

Tues 23 Sept

Started night school this evening. There are 10 of us to start with. Finished at 8.45 & came home & washed my hair. Didn't see Reg – I wonder how the Tramps Supper went?

A Tramps Supper was a social event. Participants dressed as tramps and usually ate a fish and chip supper out of newspaper.

Weds 24 Sept

Reg phoned this a.m. and said he was going to London today. I stayed in this evening & finished Win's dress – it looks very nice. Went to bed quite early. Sent Dad's card.

Thurs 25 Sept

Went straight from office to see Reg he isn't well, then dashed home & went to Liberal & Radical Club for the show. Charlie compered in Reg's place & the whole show was lousy & the audience was worse.

The Liberal and Radical Club was a working men's club in Richmond Street, Gillingham. It's likely that The Good Companions hired the premises to put on their show. The building has been refurbished and is now a mosque.

Fri 26 Sept

I went out on bantam tonight. Popped & saw Reg then went up club to tell Ken Davies Reg wouldn't be along tomorrow. Left club about 10pm because I had the bike. Went to bed quite early.

Sat 27 Sept

Went down to Reg's to tea today & went straight up club in evening to 'Top Hat'. The whole evening went off very well including our act. Came home in Pen's car with Win.

Sun 28 Sept

Went to lunch at Hoo today with Auntie Jenny and Uncle Ernest & also Uncle Walter. Auntie Audrey & Barbara came down. I left after tea & went to see Reg – played records. I was very annoyed because he didn't kiss me goodnight.

Eve's father Alfred came from a large family of five boys and two girls. Ernest and Walter were his brothers.

Mon 29 Sept

Reg phoned this a.m. and said he was feeling a little better. I went up club in evening didn't do much – sat talking to Charlie. Came home about 10.30. Didn't feel very well all day.

Tues 30 Sept

Auntie Jenny & Uncle Ernie & Auntie Audrey came to tea today. I went to night school in evening & got soaking wet. My shoes leaked & I had to sit all evening with wet feet. Went to bed early.

Weds 1 October

Reg phoned me up this a.m – I went down to see him this evening & we sat in the front room. He is no better & won't be fit to come on Friday to the dance.

According to Eve

The front room was the old fashioned parlour – the best room in the house that was kept for entertaining guests and rarely used just by the family. I remember this room from my childhood. Even though the house was small, Reg's parent used the back room as both dining and sitting room, plus for using the tin bath in front of the open coal fire as they had no bathroom.

THURS 2 OCTOBER

Popped down to see how Reg was this evening & he is about the same. Left about 8.30 & went over to Arthurs & Betty for final arrangements about tomorrow.

FRI 3 OCTOBER

Went to Folkestone to SEE Board 'Get Together' & Arthur did opening act & it went down quite well. Arrive home just after 3a.m. – very tired. Bought new pink blouse.

SEE = South Eastern Electricity – Eve's Dad's employer.

SAT 4 OCTOBER

Thank goodness it is my Saturday off! Got up at midday & stayed in all afternoon doing Ivor's coat. Went down to see Reg this evening – he had a relapse or something but seemed a bit brighter.

SUN 5 OCTOBER

Popped up club in a.m & saw Fred up there. Went to see Reg in p.m. – stayed to tea & played cards all evening. Reg seemed a lot better today. I am still crazy over him.

Mon 6 October

Went to club this evening on my bike. We had great fun, planning a new show. Nobody actually rehearsed. Came home quite early because of the bike.

Tues 7 October

Went to night school on my bike this evening. The master is a proper slave driver. Washed my hair when I came home & set it. Went to bed quite early.

Weds 8 October

Went down to see Reg this evening – he is very much better & he is growing a beard – lovely grub. I'm just glad he is getting well.

Thurs 9 October

I stayed in this evening & did some of Ivor's coat. I have nearly finished it now. Mum stayed in too & did Pam's curtains. We meant to get to bed early but didn't.

Fri 10 October

Pay day – hoorah – went out to lunch with Lorna today. I went down to see Reg this evening & he can go out tomorrow. I still love him very much – I wonder if it can last?

According to Eve

> **11 SATURDAY** s.r. 6.16, s.s. 5.149
> Reg met me from the office today & we had coffee & then went home. He came up for tea & we went to club in evening. Left early as he hasn't been out for so long. NoWP.

Sat 11 October

Reg met me from the office today & we had coffee & then went home. He came up for tea & we went to club in evening. Left early as he hasn't been out for so long. NoWP.

A reader suggested NoWP might mean 'no wild passion'. I have no other ideas!

Sun 12 October

Auntie Jenny & Uncle Ernie came to lunch today & P & M & Reg came for tea. Reg and I went to watch the baby elephants arrive & after tea we played cards.

Billy Smart's circus came to town – it was very popular at the time.

Mon 13 October.

Reg called for me this evening & we went up the club for rehearsal. The sand dance is coming along nicely now. – it is very funny. Got home just before 11pm. Reg didn't stay long.

...and we have a picture of the Sand Dance too!

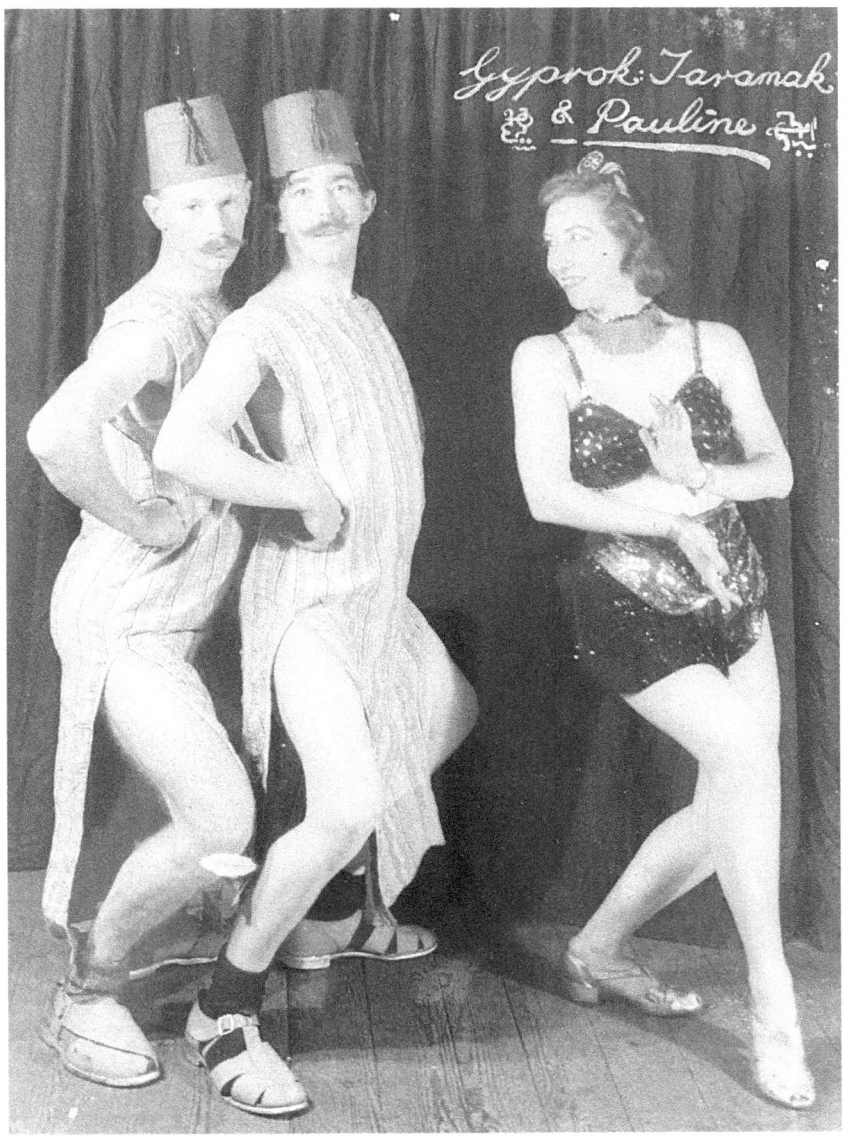

Arthur is in the middle. Image kindly provided by Lynn Armstrong (Arthur and Betty's daughter)

Tues 14 October

Went straight up club from the office today & had egg on toast – then went on to night school – Reg met me afterwards & we went down the club. I was very annoyed with Reg because we were late leaving the club.

Weds 15 October

Went up club with Reg for another rehearsal. I get very fed up sitting up there doing nothing – came home quite early.

Thurs 16 October

Went to Billie Smart's Circus on The Lines today with Reg. It was very good and we both enjoyed it. Had a drink on the way home & got in just after 10.30.

'The Lines' is short for 'The Great Lines', which is a large open space and now a Heritage Park. It sweeps up towards Gillingham from behind Chatham Town Hall. At the top of the hill there is an impressive Navy War Memorial to commemorate those that died at sea during both world wars It contains 8,515 names from World War One and a further 10,098 names from World War Two. There are identical obelisks in Plymouth and Portsmouth.

Fri 17 October

Left the office early & went to tea with Yvonne. Reg came over later in evening & we just sat talking & watching TV. Had a very pleasant evening.

Sat 18 October

I went round to see Doreen & John this p.m. & Reg & I went to club dance run by the Variety Section this evening, the band was shocking & we didn't enjoy ourselves very much.

SUN 19 OCTOBER

Went to pictures with Reg to see 'Rainbow Round My Shoulder' – was quite good. Went up the club afterwards & had tea & stayed the evening. Not too bad a day really I suppose.

'Rainbow Round my Shoulder' was an American musical starring Frankie Laine and Billy Daniels.

MON 20 OCTOBER

Work as usual today. I stayed in this evening & did my homework & washed my hair. I didn't see Reg today. I meant to go to bed early but didn't.

TUES 21 OCTOBER

I went straight from work to the club & had a meal & then on to night school. Reg met me afterwards & we went down the club – he listened to a fight & I played bar billiards with Lance.

WEDS 22 OCTOBER

Reg was late coming up this evening – we went up the club & went to the old fashioned dancing classes – it was great fun. I didn't see much of Reg – worse luck.

THURS 23 OCTOBER

According to Eve

Mum & Dad & I went over to A&B this evening & Reg came over later. Spent a very pleasant evening but I was horrible to Reg when we got home – I don't know why – we didn't part on the best of terms.

A&B are Arthur and Betty, who had agreed to provide lodgings to Eve. Eve's parents had recently been on holiday to Ramsgate. When they came home, they announced that they planned to move there. As Eve had a new job and boyfriend locally, she needed to find somewhere nearby to rent a room when the house was sold. Eve often said that she didn't leave home – home left her.

According to Eve

Eve's parents, Doris and Alfred Reed. I believe this was taken on Broadstairs promenade while they were on holiday at Ramsgate, a couple of miles away.

Fri 24 October

Popped in & saw Reg lunchtime, I think everything is still ok. I went straight from the office to Yvonne's & stayed the night. Sally nearly bit me. Yvonne is becoming a very good cook.

I assume Sally was a dog.

Sat 25 October

I stayed in all afternoon as it was raining & I didn't feel too good. Reg came up about 9 o'clock & we went over to Pete & Pat's but they weren't in so we went up the club for a little while & called in on A&B on the way home for a cup of tea.

Sun 26 October

I went to Maidstone this a.m. & then called in at club to see Reg. Reg went to meeting at club in p.m. & we met for tea at A&B's. Went up club in evening but didn't stay late.

Mon 27 October

I collected my RSA certificate today then I went up club. Reg came up just after 8pm for rehearsal. Eric was down & we had quite a chat to him. Reg is wonderful.

Tues 28 October

Went straight from office to club & then on to night school. Reg met me & we came straight home. Mum & Dad were surprised to see us so early. Reg didn't stay long.

Wed 29 October

Went up to Shirley's for tea & Roy came. Ron & Iris came in & we all sat gassing. I met Reg at Fire Station at 10 o'clock & he brought me home.

THURS 30 OCTOBER

I met Reg outside the shop tonight. & we went to The Grand to see 'An American in Paris' & 'The Bowery Boys'. They were both very good films & I enjoyed them very much.

'An American in Paris' was a popular romantic musical starring Gene Kelly and Leslie Caron that produced several hit songs.

'The Bowery Boys' are fictional New York characters who starred in forty eight comedy feature films between 1946 – 1958.

According to Eve

According to Eve

Fri 31 October

Bought brown gabardine skirt today. Reg came up in evening & we went up the club. Reg danced with me – said he was practising for tomorrow. Came home about 10.30.

Gabardine is a hardwearing, waterproof, tightly woven twill fabric invented by Thomas Burberry. It was very popular at the time, especially for jackets and outerwear.

Sat 1 November

Stayed in in p.m. as it was raining & went to a dance at Town Hall this evening with Reg. Reg was made to sing & he sung 'Walking My Baby Back Home'. It was a very good dance I enjoyed it very much.

Sun 2 November

P&M, A&B, S&R, Y&R came to tea today & we all played cards in the evening. I lost 1/3. Yvonne stayed the night & we lay talking for hours. I went out for a ride on bantam in a.m

Mon 3 November

Met Reg at the club as it was rehearsal night. Charlie didn't come so Reg couldn't rehearse. Reg & I played table tennis afterwards & I lost of course. We left club about 10.15 but Reg stayed late.

Tues 4 November

Had this p.m off from office & went for my driving test, I passed. Went to night school this evening & went down club after & saw Reg. I am thrilled that I passed my test.

According to Eve

I assume this was a motorbike test as there has been no mention of learning to drive a car.

WEDS 5 NOVEMBER

Went to Yvonne's for tea & she came down the club with me & we watched the fireworks. There was a dance after. I felt very sick coming home so Reg got a taxi – poor darling, he's so sweet.

THURS 6 NOVEMBER

Work as usual today – Reg phoned me up in p.m. I stayed in tonight & washed my hair. Went to bed about 8.45p.m.

FRI 7 NOVEMBER

Reg came up for me this morning & we went up club for rehearsal. Charlie wasn't there again so Reg couldn't rehearse. I was Duty Steward but didn't do much.

I think Eve meant evening, not morning.

SAT 8 NOVEMBER

Met Reg from the shop & went to his house for tea. In the evening we met Don Harridge at the club & went up to Eric & Cons – had a very pleasant evening – Don brought us home.

SUN 9 NOVEMBER

Reg & I stayed in in p.m. & Mum & Dad went to Hoo for tea. We went up the club in the evening. Listened to Royal Variety Show on radio in afternoon.

The Royal Variety Show was an annual event, usually attended by royalty. This was notable, as it was the first during the reign of Queen Elizabeth II. She attended, along with her husband, Prince Philip. Held at the London Palladium, the Queen declared 'This is the best show of all.' Stars appearing included popular war time singers Gracie Field and Vera Lynn and comedians Norman Wisdom and Tony Hancock. A last minute addition to the programme was the French singer Maurice Chevalier.

MON 10 NOVEMBER

Met Reg at the club this evening & Len Hill took the photos of the section. I had mine taken in the military costume. Met Arthur Kenyon on the bus & he has promised Reg a side drum.

Reg played percussion as well as singing.

TUES 11 NOVEMBER

Went up the club for tea & then to night school. I went down the club afterwards & met Reg. Came home quite early.

WEDS 12 NOVEMBER

Reg met me from work & we went to Yvonnes for tea & she came back down the club for the old time dancing. Spent quite a pleasant evening.

THURS 13 NOVEMBER

I stayed in this evening and did some of my packing. I never knew that I had so much stuff. I had a filthy headache all day & so I went to bed early.

According to Eve

Eve was packing to prepare for moving into Arthur and Betty's house.

Fri 14 November

Reg came up for me this evening & we went up the club. We sat in the lounge for a little while but didn't do very much. Came home quite early but Reg stayed until 1am.

Sat 15 November

I moved to A&B's today. Spent a hectic p.m. finishing my packing. I think I will settle in ok. We went up to watch the dress rehearsal of the 'Chiltern Hundreds' tonight. It was very good.

'The Chiltern Hundreds' was a comedy that had enjoyed a long run in the West End at The Vaudeville theatre from 1947 -49. After that, it became a popular choice with amateur drama groups. It was written by William Douglas-Home, son of Alec, a politician who became Prime Minister in 1963.

Sun 16 November

Washed my hair this morning & dried it with Betty's drier. Reg came over this p.m. for tea & we went to his house for a little while & then up to see Mum & Dad. They have been to Ramsgate for the weekend.

Mon 17 November

Reg met me up the club tonight. He's started rehearsing for the show. I played table tennis with Pete Johnson. Reg came home with me about 11o'clock. I didn't see much of him at all this evening.

According to Eve

Tues 18 November

I went home for tea & then on to night school – called in at the club on my way home & met Reg. I had egg on chips. We stayed at the club until we were thrown out this evening.

Weds 19 November

Reg met me from the office & we went to tea with Mum & Dad. They are moving tomorrow. It snowed quite a lot this evening – called in at club.

Thurs 20 November

I stayed in this evening & did a bit of ironing & mended some stockings. Reg came over & stayed to supper. I won't see him again until Sunday.

Fri 21 November

Went down to Ramsgate this evening & the house is very nice - it could be made really super. We didn't do anything this evening – just sat talking.

Sat 22 November

Scrubbed out larder for Mum and distempered the inside. Mum & I painted the passage & stairs in evening. I miss Reg most awfully & couldn't manage to get out to phone him this evening.

Sun 23 November

Distempered one bedroom this afternoon & dropped a bucket of distemper all over me. I caught the 6.30 train home & went straight to the club. Reg & I played table tennis. I lost of course.

According to Eve

MON 24 NOVEMBER

Work as usual. I did my homework after tea before I went up the club. Rehearsal went off OK this evening – Reg was pleased with it – he was busy all evening so I hardly saw him at all.

TUES 25 NOVEMBER

I didn't go to night school tonight as it was so cold. I washed my hair instead & then went up the club with Reg. We played bar billiards & table tennis & then went up in the lounge for a little while.

WEDS 26 NOVEMBER

Reg & I missed the bus to Walderslade this evening so we had to wait half an hour for next one. Stayed at Yvonnes until 9.30 then went to club & on to home.

THURS 27 NOVEMBER

I collected the mail from 60 Napier today & then went down to Betty Hatty's & saw Reg & Ted Turner & we all went up to Lens to have some more photos taken of the section.

Her parents had lived at 60 Napier Road, Gillingham

FRI 28 NOVEMBER

I met Reg up the club tonight & he & Lance organised 'I want to be an Actor'. It was very amusing. I managed to get one of the parts. Went up in the lounge with Reg afterwards.

SAT 29 NOVEMBER

Met Reg from the shop this evening & went down his house for a while – then we went up the club & sat talking in lounge until nearly midnight. A&B were in bed when I got home.

SUN 30 NOVEMBER

I helped Arthur put up decorations at club in a.m. I went up Eric & Cons in p.m. & Reg & I went back to A&B's for tea. We watched TV in evening a play called 'Adam's Apple'. It was quite good.

'Adam's Apple' by N C Hunter was shown on the BBC. It was described as 'A Victorian fairy tale in three acts.'

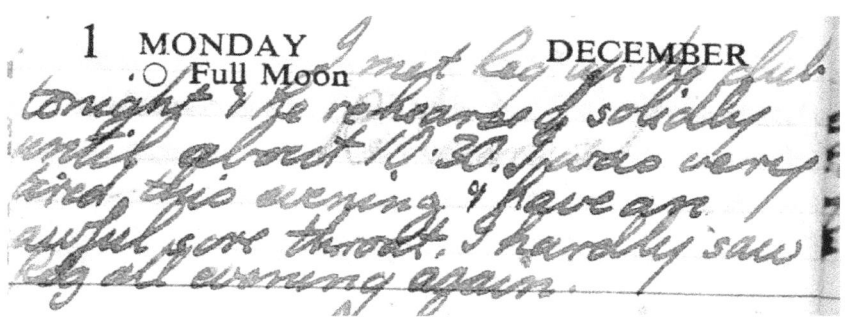

MON 1 DECEMBER

I met Reg up the club tonight & he rehearsed solidly until about 10.30. I was very tired this evening & have an awful sore throat. I hardly saw Reg all evening again.

According to Eve

Tues 2 December

I went to night school tonight & they actually had the heating on. Reg met me afterwards & we went to club – we played bar billiards & then table tennis then sat in lounge for a little while.

Weds 3 December

I went up the club early this evening & so did Reg. He had a final rehearsal. I went to the Old Time Dancing class – it was great fun. Left the club very late.

Thurs 4 December

Reg came down this evening & talked a lot about tomorrow's show. He stayed to supper & left about 11 o'clock. He is wonderful & I love him more every day.

Fri 5 December

SEE Board show at Upper Sittingbourne Conservative Club. Everything went off O.K. Myrtle went to the dinner & enjoyed the show very much.

Sat 6 December

Had my hair permed this afternoon & we did a show for the club at 7.30. There was a dance after till midnight & Reg enjoyed it very much – he sang with the band – Ken Windmills Quartette.

Sun 7 December

I met Reg in a.m & went to his home for lunch & for tea. We sat in his front room all afternoon. I love him very much. The buses stopped today because of the fog so caught train.

Mon 8 December

Was very foggy today. I went over to Gillingham to pick up Mum's club & then up to see Pam. Bought red costume today – went up club to see Reg for a little while.

Tues 9 December

Went to night school tonight & there were only 4 of us. Reg met me after & we went down to the club & played table tennis & bar billiards. I lost both of course – came home early & had a bath.

Weds 10 December

Did the show at Rainham Co-Op this evening – everything went off fine. I compered first half & we did the telepathy act in second half.

How did they appear to demonstrate mindreading? Lynn, the daughter of Arthur and Betty, found the instructions among her father's possessions. I have added them as an appendix at the back of this book – they are top secret, so if you can work out how it was done, don't tell anyone!

Thurs 11 December

I met Reg from his shop this evening & we went to the pictures – saw 2 awfully boring pictures – but it was fun just being with Reg.

According to Eve

Fri 12 December

Met Reg & Charlie at club this evening & we all went down the Naval Barracks. We did 3 acts – The Sand Dance – The 3 Chords & Telepathy. Went to the Wardroom afterwards and had whisky galore.

Sat 13 December

Met Myrtle in afternoon & we went to Lorna's church Xmas fair. We left early & I went to see Reg. Went to club to see Reg in evening – we watched TV for a while. Gosh I do love Reg.

Sun 14 December

Reg & I went up to Petticoat Lane today – we had lunch at Nell & Joe's place. Came home early & went up the club to hear Arthur Kenyon's trio. Had a wonderful day.

Petticoat Lane in Spitalfields, London has been famous for its outdoor markets since 1650.

There was a music hall artist called Arthur Kenyon. Music halls became variety shows and then dwindled in popularity after the first world war, so this may not be the same person.

Mon 15 December

I left my draw tickets at Romford & they are due in today – oh well! Reg & I went and sat in the lounge for most of the evening. We sat talking for a while & then went home quite early.

Nell and Joe lived at Romford.

Tues 16 December

I went to night school tonight – there were only 3 of us there. Reg met me outside & we went down the club. I had egg on chips – it was smashing. Played bar billiards. I lost.

Weds 17 December

Reg met me from the office today & we went out to Yvonnes for tea. We came back to club in evening but we didn't go to Old Time dancing.

Thurs 18 December

I stayed in this evening & did some mending & wrote some of my Xmas cards. I had an awful headache in evening so I went to bed early.

Fri 19 December

Arthur went away for weekend so Betty & I went up club. I saw Reg & we danced a bit in the hall & played bar billiards. Reg stayed quite late this evening until Betty got home.

Sat 20 December

I met Reg this evening & had tea at his house. We went to the Drama Dance at the club this evening – it was quite good. Betty had £3 stolen from her bag. Reg stayed late again. He's wonderful.

Sun 21 December

I went up club in a.m. & saw Reg. Went to tea at his house today. They must get fed up with seeing me. Went to pictures in evening – two awful films.

Mon 22 December

Had my hair set at lunchtime – it went quite well. Met Reg up the club this evening & we didn't stay very late.

Tues 23 December

I met Reg from his shop & we stayed in his house all evening babysitting for Brian. He tied all his presents up.

Baby Brian belonged to Nell and Joe.

Weds 24 December

Went to Xmas Eve dance at club after tea with Thrushes. Bathed Brian today! Had a wonderful evening. I love Reg so much.

Thurs 25 December

Reg & I went down to Mum & Dad in a.m. – we were late arriving had lovely grub & enjoyed everything very much. Went to bed about 2.30a.m.

Fri 26 December

Wonderful day today – took Reg a cup of tea in bed! Didn't do anything particular all day but most enjoyable. Played cards and darts in evening. Went to bed about 2 o'clock.

Sat 27 December

I got up at 5.15am & got Reg off to work on train at 6,15 a.m. At 6.40 he was back – Sunday service so he had to wait & catch 8.15. I came home in evening & went up the club with him.

Sun 28 December

Went to lunch at Reg's house & Nell, Joe & Brian went home. Reg & I dozed on sofa in p.m. & went back to A&B's for tea. We all went to see 'Monkey Business' in evening – very good film.

'Monkey Business' was a screwball American comedy. It starred Marilyn Monroe, Ginger Rogers and Cary Grant.

Tues 30 December

I didn't see Reg this evening. I pressed my dress & set my hair for tomorrow. Betty came down for a little while. I went to bed quite early.

Weds 31 December

New Years Eve. Dance tonight – it was smashing. I wore my evening dress. Reg did a show at the City Arms first. Yvonne stayed the night with me.

According to Eve

Part Three
What happened afterwards

There the diaries end. They tell us so much more than Eve's fortunes in love; they paint a social history of her life at the time. There is much that is humdrum – going to work, catching buses, attending night school – but the social life is glorious. I loved the ease of friendships they describe. If you wanted to see someone, you went to their house. If they were out, you left a note. The endless club nights and dances meant you bumped into friends and made new ones. It's a far cry from today, when we're likely to text someone to ask when a good time is to speak, and then when we do eventually arrange to meet up, we struggle to find affordable entertainment.

The accessibility of films, theatre and music seems extraordinary, or was it that Eve sought out every opportunity? If we look at her week beginning Sunday, 14 September 1952, it looks like this:

Sunday: Jazz at the Prom, Royal Albert hall, London

Monday: A friend came round

Tuesday: Cinema

Wednesday: Rehearsal at the club

Thursday: Lunch out, shopping then Norman Wisdom show at Prince of Wales theatre, Theatre, London

Friday: A dance at the NAAFI

Saturday: Visited the House of Commons and Westminster Abbey, then to the 'London Laughs' show at The Adelphi Theatre.

I don't know about you, but I've never come close to three West End shows, a dance and the cinema all in one week! Then there was The Good Companions Club, which appears to be an endless source of entertainment and activity – I can't think of anything comparable that is affordable to the working class.

On December 31st, 1952, Eve is happy and head over heels in love with Reg. The 1951 diary started on 16 January, her nineteenth birthday, when she was surrounded by friends and in love with Fred. On her twentieth, she was miserable and cried, desperate to be reunited with him. By the end of 1952, it is a couple of weeks before her twenty first birthday, which looks like a happy affair from the photographs of her party at Arthur and Betty's house.

According to Eve

Eve's 21st birthday celebration at Arthur and Betty's house.

Eve cutting her twenty first birthday cake.

Eve with Arthur at her twenty first birthday party.

But what about Fred? Eve and Fred don't seem that enamoured with each other when the diaries begin. At the beginning of 1951. Eve got bored, Fred would sometimes not show up, making excuses or leave early to go drinking. The had been together since they were sixteen. Let's not forget that Fred was only nineteen at the time, which is so young to be talking about rings and commitment.

There are discrepancies in their accounts of their relationship, too. I found out later that Fred said he went to join the army and when he came back, Mum was engaged to someone else, which appears to be an oversimplification. I had never heard mention of those difficult times when Fred was trying to win Eve back, coming round when she was already seeing Reg. Maybe being in the army changed his perspective, or maybe it was jealousy. We'll never know what they rowed about, or why Fred slapped her face and she his, leading to their breakup. Given that she seemed desperate to be back with him afterwards, I'd guess that Eve knew she had goaded him and spoken out of turn. I'm not excusing his behaviour, but I do know that Eve was a strong willed woman who would never have considered being with someone who abused her. Her tongue could be sharp, her temper and impatience sometimes getting the better of her.

Eve doesn't say that she was upset by her parent's decision to move to Ramsgate, but you'll notice there were headaches around that time, and she mentions getting cross with Reg and not knowing why. I think losing her home affected her deeply.

The house in Ramsgate that Eve's parents bought.

Eve and Reg married in July, 1954. Eve was 22 and Reg was 28. It was customary to marry in the parish of the bride's parents, and as her parents had relocated to Ramsgate, that's where the wedding was held, at St James's church.

According to Eve

Reg and Eve's wedding at St Lawrence's church, Ramsgate, in 1954.

According to Eve

I was born in 1957 followed by my sister a couple of years later. I was delighted and rather surprised to read how much Eve had loved Reg back then. I can't recall seeing any signs of affection between them when I was a child. I'd long been under the impression that I was a rebound baby, and that Fred was her one true love. She always got misty eyed at any mention of him and said that Fred was the only man that had ever dumped her

I'm sorry to say there is no Happy Ever After story. I saw no arguments between my parents – they were just Mum and Dad to me, taken for granted as parents often are. I didn't have much understanding of the state of their marriage. I do remember Eve being irritated by Reg's habit of drumming his fingers on any available surface when music was on the radio. They divorced when I was twelve. The clues, though, are in the diaries; the tiniest signs of foreboding. I wonder if readers who did not know her can spot them? Or what conclusions they drew about her character?

We can tell Eve made the most of life. Working, commuting, attending night school twice a week and making clothes for friends and family, on top of a social life that exhausts me just reading about it. She mentions being bored a couple of times. It's easy to put this down as typical teenage language but it was trait that stayed with her. She always had projects and activities on the go, including a wide variety of jobs. She was always ambitious. I remember, as a small child, having to be quiet because Mum was concentrating on doing bookkeeping for local businesses on the dining room table. There were piles of Tupperware stacked in the corner too that she sold by 'Party Plan' – a popular way for wives to make their own pin money in the 1960's.

She also writes about Reg spending a lot of time rehearsing or performing, which she sometimes begrudged. The very last entry says that Reg did a show before he came to the new Years Eve Party. This might be the biggest portent of what was to come. My father was a kind hearted, affable, man who always had a quip or a story. He was loved by many, yet music remained his first love. He held down an office job but showed little career aspiration. Every weekend he would sing with a band. They performed in clubs, had residencies in restaurants and occasionally he would front a big band and do larger concerts. (If you want to hear him sing, complete with early 60's crackle and hiss, here's a Soundcloud link: https://rb.gy/ju25gm). Mum was left at home with the children. Given her love of socialising and dancing, I doubt she was happy about that. Eventually the marriage ended in 1969.

During the mid 1970s I did a course at the local college. I met another student with the same surname as Fred – and yes, he turned out to be Fred's son. I learnt that, unsurprisingly, Fred too had married, in 1956 (not to Joan, who he dated after Eve), and started a family. I told Mum and saw the faraway look in her eyes. The old photos came out to feed her reminiscing.

Fast forward another couple of decades, and Friends Reunited became a hit – a website where you could look up all your old pals from school or college. By this time, I had married and relocated to South Lincolnshire. I looked up a few schoolmates then tried the college – and there was Fred's son. I dropped him a line and a few emails were exchanged. Fred's wife had died, and he too was now living in Lincolnshire. Eve was also single. He was about an hour away from us, but it was too much of a coincidence to ignore.

A reunion was arranged – a summer afternoon tea in our back garden. Eve was as jittery as a kitten and was so distracted that she managed to bump her car driving up the M11. It was only a minor accident, but she was nervous and shaken. It was quite out of character for her; normally she took everything in her stride.

Fred arrived, still tall and slim, maybe slightly hesitant, dressed in a khaki shirt and trousers. I could see the resemblance to his son. Polite small talk was made over cake, then we retreated and left them to catch up and share memories. They talked for hours. Mum was glowing when he left. Fred promised to keep in touch.

According to Eve

Fred and Eve's reunion in 2004.

He didn't call. The days went past, I had to stop myself from asking repeatedly if she had heard from him. Eve's disappointment was palpable. Eventually I touched base with his son and discovered that Fred had cancer. His sons believe he had had hidden it from them too, while he was undergoing treatment. It is only speculation, but possibly he hadn't wanted Eve to get close to him, only to have him leave her again. He died not long after. Mum left us in 2011, when she was 79. She had been living alone for many years.

Reg remarried when I was fifteen, to Marie, an old friend of Eve's who she had met through Tupperware, although Eve and Marie had drifted apart and not seen each other for several years. Reg and Marie bumped into each other in the High Street, struck up a conversation, went for a coffee, and the rest is history. They stayed together until he died, although I'm pretty sure his infatuation with jazz annoyed the hell out of her, too.

I was fortunate to spend his last day with him. I don't think either of my parents died with regrets, but a small piece of Mum's heart always wondered if she should have given Fred that second chance.

According to Eve

If you glean anything else from the diaries, or see things differently to me, I'd love to hear. You can find me at Twitter/X: @milla_reed , at Blue Sky: @millareed.bsky.social or on my Facebook page: Milla Reed Author

Appendix

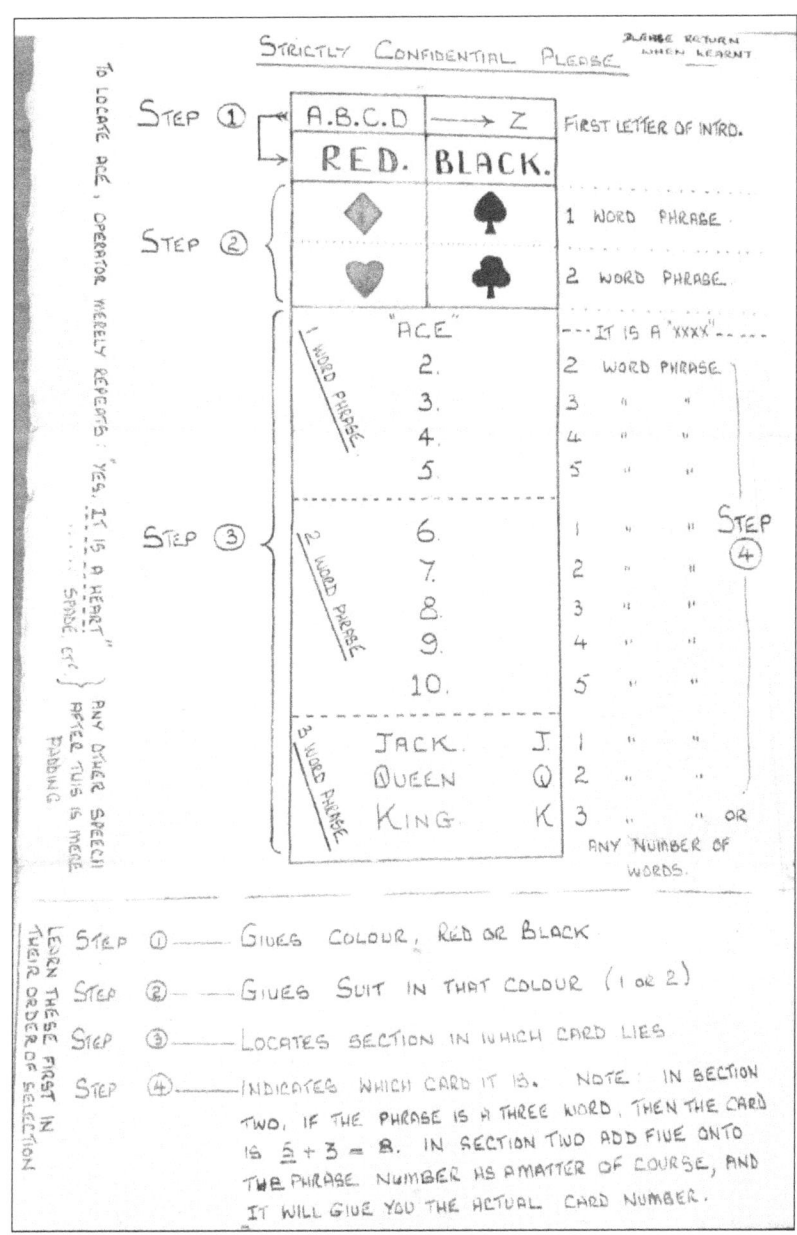

According to Eve

EXAMPLES. (IN BRIEF).

OPERATOR. (LADIES + GENTLEMEN), DURING THIS DEMONSTRATION MAY | (CLUE 1).
I ASK YOU ALL TO CONCENTRATE ON THE CARD. THANK YOU. | RED
"CONCENTRATE HARD" ② ———————————— HEART

ASST. "ITS A HEART"

OP. "YES, QUITE RIGHT. NOW WHAT SORT OF CARD IS IT ——— COURT CARD
CONCENTRATE VERY HARD" ● ③ ——————

ASST. "ITS A COURT CARD"

OP. YES,— WHICH IS IT ③ ——————————— KING
(OR — YES, CAN YOU TELL ME WHICH OF THE COURT CARDS) KING
(SEE NOTE OPPOSITE KING, OVER)

ASST. "ITS A KING"

———————————

OP. (L+G) WILL EVERYONE ETC. ETC. ————————— (W) BLACK

OP. "NOW CONCENTRATE" ② ————————————→ CLUB

ASST. ITS A CLUB.

OP. "YES. IT IS A CLUB" ————————————→ ACE

THE REMAINDER OF THE TALK IS PADDING ONLY, FOR YOU ALREADY KNOW
THAT IT IS AN ACE

———————————

(STEP ONE) (STEP TWO) (STEP THREE)
(L+G) "A CARD HAS ———— CONCENTRATE ———— THINK HARD ——
———— "AND WHAT CARD IS IT." ————.
(STEP FOUR)
ANSWER (⁵⁄₂) — [unreadable]

Thanks to Lynn Armstrong for sharing her father Arthur's secrets!

About the Author

Milla lived in the Medway towns until her twenties when she relocated to South Lincolnshire. She works as a trainer and previously published several work related books. She now lives in a village on the edge of the Cotswolds with her husband Jeremy and can often be found in the garden. She has two grown up children, who both adored their grandmother and give her credit for passing on her brains, drive and ambition. Milla's younger daughter inherited Reg's talent for singing.

She writes commercial fiction and is currently working on a novel inspired by finding her mother's diaries. If you would like to hear what Milla publishes next, please send your email address to themillareed@gmail.com.

Acknowledgements

I am indebted to so many people who have been supportive and encouraging. The first lovely souls to help were Twitter/X users who responded when I posted pictures of sentences I couldn't read from the diaries and helped me decipher them. Some of them gave me valuable feedback on early drafts – many thanks to Gill Angel, Clare Maher and Ros Coffey.

Having sorted out the words, Facebook was my next port of call. Medway History Group helped me identify some of the places and details. It was through this group that I met Lynn Armstrong, the daughter of Arthur and Betty, who feature significantly in Eve's story. Lynn helped me flesh out details about the Good Companions Club and showed me picture of my parents involved in different shows and sketches.

Fred's son, Steve, had been invaluable too. I've checked facts with him, he's told me some lovely stories about his dad's early days. I hope I've done him proud. Steve, like his dad, was a motorbike enthusiast so he got the job of clarifying which bike was which. Thank you, Steve, you're a star.

My sister, Lynne Casson, deserves a mention too. I knew there were photographs of the era, and that we wouldn't have thrown them out when Mum died. Lynne endured my nagging with good humour and finally managed to track them down in my nephew's attic.

Most of the photographs were tiny and needed professional help to get them good enough for print. Many thanks to my good friend David Bostock of David Bostock Photography for his time, patience and expertise.

Lastly, eternal thanks to my husband Jeremy Renals. He has taught me much about writing and editing as well as making endless damn fine cups of tea.

www.ingramcontent.com/pod-product-compliance
Ingram Content Group UK Ltd.
Pitfield, Milton Keynes, MK11 3LW, UK
UKHW010630251125
9165UKWH00040B/449